What Readers Are Saying About
Build Awesome Command-Line Applications in Ruby

Some command-line applications save time and are a joy to use. Others just make you want to tear your hair out. David Copeland has written a guide to writing the kind of command-line apps that will make your users want to hug you. From providing a humane command-line interface, to being self-documenting, to integrating seamlessly with the rest of the command-line universe—this book will show you how to take your scripts from adequate to awesome.

➤ Avdi Grimm
  Ruby developer, author, *Exceptional Ruby*, and blogger, Virtuous Code

This book proves that text mode is not the just the domain of batch scripts and glue code. Beyond the extensive survey of current Ruby CLI tools, David brings an unmatched focus on user experience and testing. Every full-stack developer should learn how to build the kinds of apps covered in this book.

➤ Wynn Netherland
  CTO, Pure Charity

I know of no other Ruby book that covers the content in this useful work, especially with its eye toward making Ruby command-line applications better citizens.

➤ Noel Rappin
  Senior engineer at Groupon and author, *Rails Test Prescriptions*

This well-written book teaches ideas that are really important: that Ruby is a powerful language for writing command-line tools; that CLI tools, unlike GUI tools, can be combined in an infinite number of ways; that the effort required to automate small recurrent tasks pays off; and that there are time-tested best practices for succeeding with command-line tool development. Not only are the scripts in this volume awesome, so is the book.

➤ **Staffan Nöteberg**
    Author, *Pomodoro Technique Illustrated*

I want a few people on my team to have this book now. I especially can't wait to get this in the hands of our software lead, who's a whiz at shell scripts and would be delighted to see how much easier and more reliable option parsing is in Ruby.

➤ **Ian Dees**
    Ruby developer and coauthor, *Using JRuby*

This book teaches you how to write command-line tools your mother would be proud of.

➤ **Matt Wynne**
    Independent consultant, programmer, coach, and author, *The Cucumber Book*

Build Awesome Command-Line Applications in Ruby

Control Your Computer, Simplify Your Life

David Bryant Copeland

The Pragmatic Bookshelf

Dallas, Texas • Raleigh, North Carolina

Many of the designations used by manufacturers and sellers to distinguish their products are claimed as trademarks. Where those designations appear in this book, and The Pragmatic Programmers, LLC was aware of a trademark claim, the designations have been printed in initial capital letters or in all capitals. The Pragmatic Starter Kit, The Pragmatic Programmer, Pragmatic Programming, Pragmatic Bookshelf, PragProg and the linking *g* device are trademarks of The Pragmatic Programmers, LLC.

Every precaution was taken in the preparation of this book. However, the publisher assumes no responsibility for errors or omissions, or for damages that may result from the use of information (including program listings) contained herein.

Our Pragmatic courses, workshops, and other products can help you and your team create better software and have more fun. For more information, as well as the latest Pragmatic titles, please visit us at *http://pragprog.com*.

The team that produced this book includes:

John Osborn (editor)
Potomac Indexing, LLC (indexer)
Kim Wimpsett (copyeditor)
David J Kelly (typesetter)
Janet Furlow (producer)
Juliet Benda (rights)
Ellie Callahan (support)

Printed in the United States of America.
ISBN-13: 978-1-934356-91-3
Printed on acid-free paper.
Book version: P1.0—March 2012

Contents

Introduction vii

1.   Have a Clear and Concise Purpose   1
    1.1   Problem 1: Backing Up Data   2
    1.2   Problem 2: Managing Tasks   5
    1.3   What Makes an Awesome Command-Line App   10
    1.4   Moving On   11

2.   Be Easy to Use   13
    2.1   Understanding the Command Line: Options, Arguments,
          and Commands   13
    2.2   Building an Easy-to-Use Command-Line Interface   18
    2.3   Building an Easy-to-Use Command-Suite interface   23
    2.4   Moving On   31

3.   Be Helpful   33
    3.1   Documenting a Command-Line Interface   33
    3.2   Documenting a Command Suite   38
    3.3   Including a Man Page   42
    3.4   Writing Good Help Text and Documentation   47
    3.5   Moving On   50

4.   Play Well with Others   53
    4.1   Using Exit Codes to Report Success or Failure   54
    4.2   Using the Standard Output and Error Streams
          Appropriately   59
    4.3   Formatting Output for Use As Input to Another
          Program   63
    4.4   Trapping Signals Sent from Other Apps   68
    4.5   Moving On   69

5. **Delight Casual Users** 71
    5.1 Choosing Names for Options and Commands   72
    5.2 Choosing Default Values for Flags and Arguments   76
    5.3 Deciding Default Behavior   82
    5.4 Moving On   86

6. **Make Configuration Easy** 89
    6.1 Why External Configuration?   89
    6.2 Reading External Configuration from Files   90
    6.3 Using Configuration Files with Command Suites   94
    6.4 Design Considerations When Using Configuration   98
    6.5 Moving On   99

7. **Distribute Painlessly** 101
    7.1 Distributing with RubyGems   101
    7.2 Distributing Without RubyGems   108
    7.3 Collaborating with Other Developers   109
    7.4 Moving On   115

8. **Test, Test, Test** 117
    8.1 Testing User Behavior with Acceptance Tests   118
    8.2 Testing in Isolation with Unit Tests   131
    8.3 A Word About Test-Driven Development   139
    8.4 Moving On   139

9. **Be Easy to Maintain** 141
    9.1 Dividing Code into Multiple Files   141
    9.2 Designing Code for Maintainability   146
    9.3 Moving On   151

10. **Add Color, Formatting, and Interactivity** 153
    10.1 Adding Color Using ANSI Escape Sequences   154
    10.2 Formatting Output with Tables   159
    10.3 Providing Interactive User Input with readline   164
    10.4 Moving On   173

A1. **Common Command-Line Gems and Libraries** 175
    A1.1 Alternatives for Simple Command-Line Apps   176
    A1.2 Alternatives for Command Suites   184
    A1.3 Other Relevant Libraries   189

A2. **Bibliography** 193

     Index 195

Introduction

Graphical user interfaces (GUIs) are great for a lot of things; they are typically much kinder to newcomers than the stark glow of a cold, blinking cursor. This comes at a price: you can get only so proficient at a GUI before you have to learn its esoteric keyboard shortcuts. Even then, you will hit the limits of productivity and efficiency. GUIs are notoriously hard to script and automate, and when you can, your script tends not to be very portable.

This is all beside the point; we are software developers, and we write programs. What could be more natural than using code to get our work done? Consider the following command sequence:

```
> cd ~/Projects/cli
> vi chapter2.md
```

While these two commands might strike you as opaque, they are a highly efficient means of editing a file.

For most of my career, the command line meant a UNIX shell, like bash. The bash shell provides some basic built-in commands, as well as access to many other standard (and nonstandard) commands that are shipped with any UNIX system. These commands are single-purpose, require no user interaction, and come with easy-to-use (but hard-to-learn) user interfaces. These attributes let you piece them together in a near-infinite number of ways. Automating sophisticated behavior, performing complicated analysis, and parsing a myriad of text files can be done easily and expediently. This was life for me early on in my career. And it was good.

Then, in the mid-1990s, as Java grew in popularity, the idea of stringing together UNIX command-line utilities to get things done came to be seen as archaic. Java programs eschewed simple text-based configuration and file-based input/output (I/O) for complex hierarchies of XML driven by RPC and HTTP I/O. This allowed for very sophisticated systems to be built, and GUI tools sprang up to abstract away the complexity of building and configuring these systems. Even the act of writing and building code got swallowed up by ever more complex integrated development environments (IDEs). The simplicity of the command line was starting to get lost.

The problem is, there are too many tasks that don't fit the model of these tools; it's just too darn easy to go out to the shell and get things done. So, while I never bought into the concept that IDEs and sophisticated GUI tools were an advancement of the command line, I made peace with the facts of life and settled into a comfortable pattern: Java was for "real" code, and the command line (along with Perl and Ruby) was for automation, one-off scripts, and other things that helped me get repetitive things done quickly.

In the mid 2000s, I started to take notice of Ruby, Rails, and the amazing community built up around these tools. To my surprise (and delight), almost everything was command-line driven. Dynamic languages like Ruby don't lend themselves too well to IDEs (some even argue that an IDE makes no sense for such languages), and the burgeoning developer community wasn't on the radar of any top-tier tool makers. The community embraced the command line and created command-line applications for everything. Although Perl had been doing this for years, this was the first time I'd noticed such a strong embrace of the command line in the "post-Java" world.

What was more interesting was the taste and polish put into these command-line apps. Most featured a full-blown help system, often with command-based navigation of features, but still stayed true to the "UNIX way" of simplicity and interoperability. Take gem, for example. It's the command used to install other Ruby apps and libraries into your system:

```
$ gem help
RubyGems is a sophisticated package manager for Ruby.  This is a
basic help message containing pointers to more information.

  Usage:
    gem -h/--help
    gem -v/--version
    gem command [arguments...] [options...]

  Examples:
    gem install rake
    gem list --local
    gem build package.gemspec
    gem help install

  Further help:
    gem help commands            list all 'gem' commands
    gem help examples            show some examples of usage
    gem help platforms           show information about platforms
```

```
    gem help <COMMAND>          show help on COMMAND
                                  (e.g. 'gem help install')
    gem server                 present a web page at
                               http://localhost:8808/
                               with info about installed gems
  Further information:
    http://rubygems.rubyforge.org
```

This is just a small part of the very complete documentation available, and it's all there, right from the command line. It's clear that a lot of thought was put into making this tool polished; this was no one-off, hacky script. Much like the design philosophy of Ruby on Rails, there was clear care given to the user experience of the programmer. These tools aren't one-off scripts someone pieced together; they are made for "real" work.

What this told me was that the command line is far from the anachronism that Java tool vendors would have us believe; it's here to stay. The future of development won't just be manipulating buttons and toolbars and dragging and dropping icons to create code; the efficiency and productivity inherent to a command-line interface will always have a place in a good developer's tool chest. There are developers who demand polish and usability from their command-line tools, and there are developers who are interested in delivering it!

That's what this book is about: delivering awesome command-line applications (and how easy it is to do so in Ruby). It's for any programmer who wants to unlock the potential of a command-line interface but who also wants to create a polished and robust application with a real user interface that is easy to grasp and use.

How This Book Is Organized

In the next ten chapters, we'll discuss every detail of command-line application development, from user input, program output, and code organization to error handling, testing, and distribution. We'll learn about this by building and enhancing two example applications. Over the course of the book, we'll make them better and better to learn what an awesome command-line app is. We'll see that Ruby makes it very easy to do, thanks to its great syntax and features, as well as several open source libraries.

The first thing we'll learn—in Chapter 1, *Have a Clear and Concise Purpose*, on page 1—is what sort of applications are right for the command line. We'll then learn—in Chapter 2, *Be Easy to Use*, on page 13—the nuts and bolts of making an awesome application that's easy for both users and the system to interact with. That chapter is all about the user interface of command-line apps and introduces the two main styles of app: a simple UNIX-like style and the more complex "command-suite" style, as exemplified by commands like git or gem.

In Chapter 3, *Be Helpful*, on page 33, we'll learn how to provide excellent help and usage documentation; command-line apps are harder to discover and learn compared to GUIs, so this is one of the most important things to get right. We'll follow that up with Chapter 4, *Play Well with Others*, on page 53, where we'll learn how to make our apps interoperable with any other system.

At this point, we'll know how to make a *good* command-line app. Chapter 5, *Delight Casual Users*, on page 71 is where we take things to the next level and learn how easy it is to add polish to our apps. We'll continue this trend in Chapter 6, *Make Configuration Easy*, on page 89, where we'll learn how to make our apps easy to use for users with many different tastes and preferences.

Chapter 7, *Distribute Painlessly*, on page 101 will cover everything you need to distribute your application with RubyGems so that others can use it (we'll also cover installation in tightly controlled environments where RubyGems isn't an option).

In Chapter 8, *Test, Test, Test*, on page 117, we'll learn all about testing command-line apps, including some techniques to keep your tests from making a mess of your system. With the ability to test our apps comes the ability to refactor them so they are easier to maintain and enhance. Chapter 9, *Be Easy to Maintain*, on page 141 will cover some conventions around code organization, as well as some design patterns that are most useful to command-line apps.

We'll finish by pushing the envelope of what command-line apps should do in Chapter 10, *Add Color, Formatting, and Interactivity*, on page 153. We'll learn all about colored, formatted output, as well as interacting with the user using Readline.

Many open source libraries and tools help make command-line apps in Ruby. We'll look at some of them, such as OptionParser, GLI, and Cucumber, in great detail. But you don't have to limit yourself to just these tools. Appendix 1, *Common Command-Line Gems and Libraries*, on page 175 will go over many of the other popular libraries so you can use the best tool for you.

Who This Book Is For

This book is aimed at both developers and system administrators who have some familiarity with Ruby and who find themselves automating things on the command line (or who wish they could).

- If you're a developer who finds yourself faced with automation tasks but aren't familiar with the various conventions and techniques around the command line, this book will help you. A problem you might have is the maintenance of a "quick hack" script you wrote that has lived long past its prime. This book will give you the tools and techniques to make your next script longer-lived, polished, and bulletproof...all without spending a lot of time on it.

- If you're a sysadmin, you might find shell scripting limiting or frustrating. If you're pushing bash to the limit in your automation tasks, this book will open up a whole new world for you. Writing command-line apps in Ruby is also a great way to really learn Ruby and become a better programmer, since you can apply it directly to your day-to-day tasks.

What You'll Need

The only thing you'll need to follow along is a Ruby installation and a UNIX-like shell. Ruby 1.9.2 or greater is recommended; however, the examples should work fine with 1.8.7 (we'll let you know if there's an important difference you need to be aware of). If you download the code from the book's website,[1] you'll notice at the top of the archive is a Gemfile. This should contain a list of all the gems you need to run the example apps, and you can use this file, along with Bundler,[2] to install everything in one step. If you don't know what any of that means, don't worry; the book will tell you when to install any needed gems. If things aren't working right, you can use the Gemfile to see which versions of gems I used when writing the book.

For writing command-line apps and following along with the examples, Mac and Linux users just need a text editor and a terminal or shell application (I'm assuming you'll have Ruby installed already; most Linux distributions include it). I highly recommend that you use RVM[3] and create a gemset for the examples in this book. RVM allows you to install any version of Ruby

---

1. http://pragprog.com/book/dccar/build-awesome-command-line-applications-in-ruby
2. http://gembundler.com
3. http://beginrescueend.com

alongside your system version and to isolate gems from one another, which is very handy when learning new technologies.

For Windows users, the examples and code should work from the command prompt; however, you might have a better experience installing Cygwin[4] or MSYS[5] and using one of those for your shell. If you haven't installed Ruby, the easiest way to do that is to use the Ruby Installer.[6] For the most part, everything in this book is compatible with Windows, with the exception of the following:

- For apps with the suffix .rb, you will need to associate the file extension with Ruby. You should be able to do this when running the Ruby Installer. For apps that have no suffix, assuming you've set up the association to the .rb extension, you will need to run the app via the ruby command, like so:

```
c:\> ruby my_app.rb
```

  To simplify things, you could create a .bat file to wrap this up:

```
@echo off
ruby my_app.rb %*
```

  The %* ensures that all the command-line parameters you give to your .bat will get passed along to your app.

- Aruba, the tool we'll be using to run acceptance tests of our command-line apps, is not well supported on Windows at the time of this writing. We'll cover this in more detail when we get to the chapter on testing, which is Chapter 8, *Test, Test, Test*, on page 117.

Other than that, if there's something a Windows user will need to do a bit differently, we'll point it out, but generally speaking, things work well on both UNIX-like platforms and Windows.

Conventions Used in the Book

There are three important things to know about the layout and conventions used in this book: the level of background knowledge you'll need on Ruby, UNIX, and OO; the way we'll work with code; and where testing fits into all this.

---

4. http://www.cygwin.com/
5. http://www.mingw.org/wiki/MSYS
6. http://rubyinstaller.org/

Ruby, UNIX, and Object Orientation

Since this is a book about writing command-line apps in Ruby, you're going to need to know a bit about the Ruby language and the UNIX environment. We've kept the code examples as clear as we can so that even with a passing familiarity with Ruby and UNIX, you'll be able to follow along.

Later in the book, we'll start to use more of the object-oriented features of Ruby, so knowing what classes and objects are will be helpful. Again, we've kept it as simple as we could so you can focus on the tools and techniques without getting distracted by some of Ruby's more esoteric features.

If you're very new to Ruby or just want to brush up, please consider the Ruby Koans[7] and the "Pickaxe Book" (*Programming Ruby: The Pragmatic Programmer's Guide* [TFH09]).

Code

It's also worth pointing out that this book is about *code*. There is a lot of code, and we'll do our best to take each new bit of it step by step. Much of the code in this book will be from two example applications that we'll enhance and improve over time. To point out new things that we're changing, we'll use a subtle but important callout. Consider some Ruby code like so:

```
if !filename.nil?
  File.open(filename) do |file|
    file.readlines do |line|
      puts line.upcase
    end
  end
end
```

We might want to change that if to an unless to avoid the negative test.

```
➤ unless filename.nil?
  File.open(filename) do |file|
    file.readlines do |line|
      puts line.upcase
    end
  end
end
```

Do you see the arrow next to the new unless statement? Look for those every time there's new code. Occasionally, we'll introduce a larger change to the code we're working on. In those cases, we'll call out particular lines for reference, like so:

7. http://rubykoans.com/

```
① def upper_case_file(filename)
②   unless filename.nil?
      File.open(filename) do |file|
        file.readlines do |line|
③         puts line.upcase
        end
      end
    end
  end
```

We can then discuss particular lines using a numbered list:

① Here we define a new method named upper_case_file.

② We check for nil here, so we don't get an exception from File.open.

③ Finally, we uppercase the line we read from the file before printing it with puts.

Testing

The Ruby community loves testing; test-driven development is at the heart of many great Ruby applications, and the community has a wide variety of tools to make testing very easy. We'll even be looking at some in Chapter 8, *Test, Test, Test*, on page 117. We won't, however, be doing much testing until then. While you should absolutely test everything you do, it can be somewhat distracting to explain a concept or best practice in the context of a unit test, especially with some of the unique features and challenges of a command-line application.

So, don't take the lack of testing as an endorsement of cowboy coding.[8]. We're omitting the tests so you can take in the important parts of making an awesome command-line application. Once you're comfortable with these best practices, the information we'll discuss about testing will leave you with all the skills you need to test-drive your next command-line app.

Online Resources

At the website for this book,[9] you'll find the following:

• The full source code for all the sample programs used in this book.

• An errata page, listing any mistakes in the current edition (let's hope that will be empty!).

---

8. http://en.wikipedia.org/wiki/Cowboy_coding
9. http://pragprog.com/titles/dccar

- A discussion forum where you can communicate directly with the author and other Ruby developers. You are free to use the source code in your own applications as you see fit.

Note: If you're reading the ebook, you can also click the little gray rectangle before the code listings to download that source file directly.

Acknowledgments

This book started as part of the Pragmatic Programmers' "PragProWriMo," which isn't much more than some budding authors posting their daily writing stats to a forum[10] every day during the month of November. This book is very different from the 170 pages I produced in November 2010, but I wrote almost every day, proving that I could actually produce a book's worth of material and that writing command-line applications in Ruby was a large enough topic to fill a book!

I had no particular plans to do anything with the manuscript I wrote, but when Travis Swicegood, author of *Pragmatic Version Control with Git* [Swi08], posted in the forum that his PragProWriMo manuscript had been accepted for development, I thought I'd submit mine as well. So, while Travis wasn't the inspiration for the material in this book, he certainly was the inspiration for turning this material *into* a book.

There are a lot of people to thank, but I have to start with my wife, Amy, who has been amazingly supportive and encouraging. She even let me install Ruby, vim, and Cygwin on her Windows laptop for testing.

I'd like to thank my editor, John Osborn, for his patience and advice as well as for inadvertently giving me a crash course in technical writing.

Next, I'd like to thank all the technical reviewers who gave me invaluable feedback on my manuscript at various stages of its development. They include Paul Barry, Daniel Bretoi, Trevor Burnham, Ian Dees, Avdi Grimm, Wynn Netherland, Staffan Nöteberg, Noel Rappin, Eric Sendlebach, Christopher Sexton, and Matt Wynne.

Finally, I'd like to thank the many programmers who've contributed to the open source projects I mention in the book, including, but probably not limited to, the following: Aslak Hellesøy, TJ Holowaychuk, Ara Howard, Yehuda Katz, James Mead, William Morgan, Ryan Tomayko, Chris Wanstrath, and,

---

10. http://forums.pragprog.com/forums/190

of course Yukihiro "Matz" Matsumoto, who created such a wonderful language in which to write command-line apps.

With all that being said, let's get down to business and start making our command-line apps a lot more awesome!

## CHAPTER 1

Have a Clear and Concise Purpose

You need to solve a problem. It might be that you need two systems to talk to each other that weren't designed for it. Or you may need to run some automated yet complex task periodically. Or, you may want to build simple productivity tools to help you work. This is where the command line shines, and these are the kinds of problems you'll learn to solve in this book.

Although it may seem obvious that a focused, single-purpose app is more desirable than one with a "kitchen sink" full of features, it's especially important for command-line apps. The way in which command-line apps get input, are configured, and produce output is incredibly simple and, in some ways, limiting. As such, a system of many single-purpose apps is better than a system of fewer (or one) complex apps. Simple, single-purpose apps are easier to understand, are easier to learn, are easier to maintain, and lead to more flexible systems.

Think of your command-line tasks as a set of layers: with the basic foundation of the standard UNIX tools, you can create more complex but still focused command-line apps. Those can be used for even more complex apps, each built on simpler tools below. The popular version control system git follows this design: many of git's commands are "plumbing" and are not intended for regular use. These commands are then used to build "porcelain" commands, which are still simple and single-purpose but are built using the "plumbing." This design comes in handy because, every once in a while, you need to use the "plumbing" directly. You can do this because git was designed around tools that each have a clear and concise purpose.

This chapter will set the stage for everything we'll be learning in the book. We'll look at two common problems and introduce two command-line apps to solve them. As a means of demonstrating more clearly what we mean by having a "clear and concise purpose," each problem-solving app will get an iteration in this chapter. The first version of each app will be naive and then quickly revised to be more single-purpose, so we can see firsthand the level of function we want our apps to have.

1.1 Problem 1: Backing Up Data

Suppose our small development team is starting work on our company's flagship web application. This application is heavily data-driven and highly complex, with many features and edge cases. To build it, we're going to use an Agile methodology, where we work in two-week "sprints." In each sprint, we'll have a list of "user stories" representing the work we're doing. To officially complete a user story, we'll need to demonstrate that story functioning properly in a shared development environment.

To be able to demonstrate working features, we'll have a set of databases with specially chosen data that can simulate all of our edge cases and user flows. Setting up this data is time-consuming because our app is complex, so even though this data is fake, we want to treat it like real production data and back it up. Since we're constantly changing the data as we work, we want to save the state of each database every single day of the current iteration. We also want to keep a backup of the state of each database at the end of every iteration. So, if we're on the fifth day of our third iteration, we want to be able to access a backup for iterations 1 and 2, as well as backups for the first four days of the third iteration.

Like with most teams, at our company, we can't rely on a system administrator to back it up for us; we're a fledgling start-up, and resources are limited. A command-line app to the rescue! We need an app that will do the following:

- Do a complete dump of any MySQL database
- Name the backup file based on the date of the backup
- Allow the creation of our "end-of-iteration" backup, using a different naming scheme
- Compress the backup files
- Delete backups from completed iterations

Let's take a quick stab at it. We'll set up a Hash that contains information about all the databases we want to back up, loop over it, and then use Ruby's backtick operator to call mysqldump, followed by gzip. We'll also examine the first argument given to our app; if it's present, we'll take that to mean we want to do an "end-of-iteration" backup. Here's what our initial implementation looks like:

```
have_a_purpose/db_backup/bin/db_backup_initial.rb
#!/usr/bin/env ruby

databases = {
  :big_client => {
    :database => 'big_client',
    :username => 'big',
    :password => 'big',
  },
  :small_client => {
    :database => 'small_client',
    :username => 'small',
    :password => 'p@ssWord!',
  }
}

end_of_iter = ARGV.shift

databases.each do |name,config|
  if end_of_iter.nil?
    backup_file = config[:database] + '_' + Time.now.strftime('%Y%m%d')
  else
    backup_file = config[:database] + '_' + end_of_iter
  end
  mysqldump = "mysqldump -u#{config[:username]} -p#{config[:password]} " +
    "#{config[:database]}"

  `#{mysqldump} > #{backup_file}.sql`
  `gzip #{backup_file}.sql`
end
```

If you're wondering what's going on the very first line, see *Shebang: How the System Knows an App Is a Ruby Script*, on page 4. Notice how we use ARGV, which is an Array that Ruby sets with all the command-line arguments to detect whether this is an "end-of-iteration" backup. In that case, we assume that whatever the argument was should go into the filename, instead of the current date. We'd call it like so:

```
$ db_backup_initial.rb
# => creates big_client_20110103.sql.gz
# => creates small_client_20110103.sql.gz
$ db_backup_initial.rb iteration_3
# => creates big_client_iteration_3.sql.gz
# => creates small_client_iteration_3.sql.gz
```

There are a lot of problems with this app and lots of room for improvement. The rest of the book will deal with these problems, but we're going to solve the biggest one right now. This app doesn't have a clear and concise purpose.

Shebang: How the System Knows an App Is a Ruby Script

Compiled programs include information in the executable file that tells that operating system how to start the program. Since programs written in a scripting language, like Ruby, don't need to be compiled, the operating system must have some other way to know how to run these types of apps. On UNIX systems, this is done via the first line of code, commonly referred to as the *shebang*.[a]

The shebang starts with a number sign (#), followed by an exclamation point (!), followed by the path to an interpreter that will be used to execute the program. This path must be an absolute path, and this requirement can cause problems on some systems. Suppose we have a simple app like so:

```
#!/usr/bin/ruby
puts "Hello World!"
```

For this app to work on any other system, there must be a Ruby interpreter located at /usr/bin/ruby. This might not be where Ruby is installed, and for systems that use RVM (an increasingly high number do so), Ruby will *never* be available in /usr/bin.

To solve this, the program /usr/bin/env, which is much more likely to be installed at that location, can be used to provide a level of indirection. env takes an argument, which is the name of a command to run. It searches the path for this command and runs it. So, we can change our program to use a shebang like so:

```
#!/usr/bin/env ruby
puts "Hello world!"
```

This way, as long as Ruby is in our path somewhere, the app will run fine. Further, since the number sign is the comment character for Ruby, the shebang is ignored if you execute your app with Ruby directly: ruby my_app.rb.

---

a. http://en.wikipedia.org/wiki/Shebang_(Unix)

It may appear to—after all, it is backing up and compressing our databases —but let's imagine a likely scenario: adding a third database to back up.

To support this, we'd need to edit the code, modify the databases Hash, and redeploy the app to the database server. We need to make this app simpler. What if it backed up only *one* database? If it worked that way, we would call the app one time for each database, and when adding a third database for backup, we'd simply call it a third time. No source code changes or redistribution needed.

To make this change, we'll get the database name, username, and password from the command line instead of an internal Hash, like this:

```
have_a_purpose/db_backup/bin/db_backup.rb
#!/usr/bin/env ruby
database = ARGV.shift
username = ARGV.shift
password = ARGV.shift
end_of_iter = ARGV.shift
if end_of_iter.nil?
  backup_file = database + Time.now.strftime("%Y%m%d")
else
  backup_file = database + end_of_iter
end
`mysqldump -u#{username} -p#{password} #{database} > #{backup_file}.sql`
`gzip #{backup_file}.sql`
```

Now, to perform our backup, we call it like so:

```
$ db_backup.rb big_client big big
# => creates big_client_20110103.sql.gz
$ db_backup.rb small_client small "p@ssWord!"
# => creates small_client_20110103.sql.gz
$ db_backup.rb big_client big big iteration_3
# => creates big_client_iteration_3.sql.gz
$ db_backup.rb medium_client medium "med_pass" iteration_4
# => creates medium_client_iteration_4.sql.gz
```

It may seem like we've complicated things, but our app is a lot simpler now and therefore easier to maintain, enhance, and understand. To set up our backups, we'd likely use cron (which is a UNIX tool for regularly scheduling things to be run) and have it run our app three times, once for each database.

We'll improve on db_backup.rb throughout the book, turning it into an awesome command-line app. Of course, automating specialized tasks is only one use of the command line. The command line can also be an excellent interface for simple productivity tools. As developers, we tend to be on the command line a lot, whether editing code, running a build, or testing new tools. Given that, it's nice to be able to manage our work without leaving the command line.

1.2   Problem 2: Managing Tasks

Most software development organizations use some sort of task management or trouble-ticket system. Tools like JIRA, Bugzilla, and Pivotal Tracker provide a wealth of features for managing the most complex workflows and tasks, all from your web browser. A common technique when programming is to take a large task and break it down into smaller tasks, possibly even breaking *those* tasks down. Suppose we're working on a new feature for our company's flagship web application. We're going to add a Terms of Service page and need to modify the account sign-up page to require that the user accept the new terms of service.

In our company-wide task management tool, we might see a task like "Add Terms of Service Checkbox to Signup Page." That's the perfect level of granularity to track the work by our bosses and other interested stakeholders, but it's too coarse to drive our work. So, we'll make a task list of what needs to be done:

- Add new field to database for "accepted terms on date."
- Get DBA approval for new field.
- Add checkbox to HTML form.
- Add logic to make sure the box is checked before signing up is complete.
- Perform peer code review when all work is done.

Tracking such fine-grained and short-lived tasks in our web-based task manager is going to be too cumbersome. We could write this on a scrap of paper or a text file, but it would be better to have a simple tool to allow us to create, list, and complete tasks in order. That way, any time we come back to our computer, we can easily see how much progress we've made and what's next to do.

To keep things single-purpose, we'll create three command-line apps, each doing the one thing we need to manage tasks. todo-new.rb will let us add a new task, todo-list.rb will list our current tasks, and todo-done.rb will complete a task.

They will all work off a shared text file, named todo.txt in the current directory, and work like so:

```
$ todo-new.rb "Add new field to database for 'accepted terms on date'"
Task added
$ todo-new.rb "Get DBA approval for new field."
Task added
$ todo-list.rb
1 - Add new field to database for 'accepted terms on date'
    Created:   2011-06-03 13:45
2 - Get DBA approval for new field.
    Created:   2011-06-03 13:46
$ todo-done.rb 1
Task 1 completed
$ todo-list.rb
1 - Add new field to database for 'accepted terms on date'
    Created:   2011-06-03 13:45
    Completed: 2011-06-03 14:00
2 - Get DBA approval for new field.
    Created:   2011-06-03 13:46
```

We'll start with todo-new.rb, which will read in the task from the command line and append it to todo.txt, along with a timestamp.

have_a_purpose/todo/bin/todo-new.rb
```ruby
#!/usr/bin/env ruby

new_task = ARGV.shift

File.open('todo.txt','a') do |file|
  file.puts "#{new_task},#{Time.now}"
  puts "Task added."
end
```

This is pretty straightforward; we're using a comma-separated-values format for the file that stores our tasks. todo-list.rb will now read that file, printing out what it finds and generating the ID number.

have_a_purpose/todo/bin/todo-list.rb
```ruby
#!/usr/bin/env ruby

File.open('todo.txt','r') do |file|
  counter = 1
  file.readlines.each do |line|
    name,created,completed = line.chomp.split(/,/)
    printf("%3d - %s\n",counter,name)
    printf("      Created   : %s\n",created)
    unless completed.nil?
      printf("      Completed : %s\n",completed)
    end
    counter += 1
  end
end
```

Finally, for todo-done.rb, we'll read the file in and write it back out, stopping when we get the task the user wants to complete and including a timestamp for the completed date as well:

have_a_purpose/todo/bin/todo-done.rb
```ruby
#!/usr/bin/env ruby

task_number = ARGV.shift.to_i

File.open('todo.txt','r') do |file|
  File.open('todo.txt.new','w') do |new_file|
    counter = 1
    file.readlines.each do |line|
      name,created,completed = line.chomp.split(/,/)
      if task_number == counter
        new_file.puts("#{name},#{created},#{Time.now}")
        puts "Task #{counter} completed"
```

```
    else
      new_file.puts("#{name},#{created},#{completed}")
    end
    counter += 1
  end
 end
end
`mv todo.txt.new todo.txt`
```

As with db_backup_initial.rb, this set of command-line apps has some problems. The most important, however, is that we've gone too far making apps clear and concise. We have three apps that share a lot of logic. Suppose we want to add a new field to our tasks. We'll have to make a similar change to all three apps to do it, and we'll have to take extra care to keep them in sync.

Let's turn this app into a *command suite*. A command suite is an app that provides a set of commands, each representing a different function of a related concept. In our case, we want an app named todo that has the clear and concise purpose of managing tasks but that does so through a command-style interface, like so:

```
$ todo new "Add new field to database for 'accepted terms on date'"
Task added
$ todo new "Get DBA approval for new field."
Task added
$ todo list
1 - Add new field to database for 'accepted terms on date'
    Created:   2011-06-03 13:45
2 - Get DBA approval for new field.
    Created:   2011-06-03 13:46
$ todo done 1
Task 1 completed
$ todo list
1 - Add new field to database for 'accepted terms on date'
    Created:   2011-06-03 13:45
    Completed: 2011-06-03 14:00
2 - Get DBA approval for new field.
    Created:   2011-06-03 13:46
```

The invocation syntax is almost identical, except that we can now keep all the code in one file. What we'll do is grab the first element of ARGV and treat that as the command. Using a case statement, we'll execute the proper code for the command. But, unlike the previous implementation, which used three files, because we're in one file, we can share some code, namely, the way in which we read and write our tasks to the file.

have_a_purpose/todo/bin/todo

```ruby
#!/usr/bin/env ruby

TODO_FILE = 'todo.txt'

def read_todo(line)
  line.chomp.split(/,/)
end

def write_todo(file,name,created=Time.now,completed='')
  file.puts("#{name},#{created},#{completed}")
end

command = ARGV.shift

case command
when 'new'
  new_task = ARGV.shift

  File.open(TODO_FILE,'a') do |file|
    write_todo(file,new_task)
    puts "Task added."
  end
when 'list'
  File.open(TODO_FILE,'r') do |file|
    counter = 1
    file.readlines.each do |line|
      name,created,completed = read_todo(line)
      printf("%3d - %s\n",counter,name)
      printf("      Created   : %s\n",created)
      unless completed.nil?
        printf("      Completed : %s\n",completed)
      end
      counter += 1
    end
  end
when 'done'
  task_number = ARGV.shift.to_i

  File.open(TODO_FILE,'r') do |file|
    File.open("#{TODO_FILE}.new",'w') do |new_file|
      counter = 1
      file.readlines.each do |line|
        name,created,completed = read_todo(line)
        if task_number == counter
          write_todo(new_file,name,created,Time.now)
          puts "Task #{counter} completed"
        else
          write_todo(new_file,name,created,completed)
        end
```

```
          counter += 1
        end
      end
    end
    `mv #{TODO_FILE}.new #{TODO_FILE}`
end
```

Notice how the methods read_todo and write_todo encapsulate the format of tasks in our file? If we ever needed to change them, we can do it in just one place. We've also put the name of the file into a constant (TODO_FILE), so that can easily be changed as well.

1.3   What Makes an Awesome Command-Line App

Since the rest of this book is about what makes an awesome command-line app, it's worth seeing a broad overview of what we're talking about. In general, an awesome command-line app has the following characteristics:

Easy to use
> The command-line can be an unforgiving place to be, so the easier an app is to use, the better.

Helpful
> Being easy to use isn't enough; the user will need clear direction on *how* to use an app and how to fix things they might've done wrong.

Plays well with others
> The more an app can interoperate with other apps and systems, the more useful it will be, and the fewer special customizations that will be needed.

Has sensible defaults but is configurable
> Users appreciate apps that have a clear goal and opinion on how to do something. Apps that try to be all things to all people are confusing and difficult to master. Awesome apps, however, allow advanced users to tinker under the hood and use the app in ways not imagined by the author. Striking this balance is important.

Installs painlessly
> Apps that can be installed with one command, on any environment, are more likely to be used.

Fails gracefully
> Users will misuse apps, trying to make them do things they weren't designed to do, in environments where they were never designed to run. Awesome apps take this in stride and give useful error messages without

being destructive. This is because they're developed with a comprehensive test suite.

Gets new features and bug fixes easily
Awesome command-line apps aren't awesome just to use; they are awesome to hack on. An awesome app's internal structure is geared around quickly fixing bugs and easily adding new features.

Delights users
Not all command-line apps have to output monochrome text. Color, formatting, and interactive input all have their place and can greatly contribute to the user experience of an awesome command-line app.

1.4 Moving On

The example apps we saw in this chapter don't have many aspects of an awesome command-line app. They're downright awful, in fact, but we have to start somewhere, and these are simple enough and general enough that we can demonstrate everything we need to know about making an awesome command-line app by enhancing them.

In this chapter, we learned the absolute most important thing for a command-line app: have a clear, concise purpose that solves a problem we have. Next, we'll learn how to make our app easier to use by implementing a more canonical command-line interface. As we work through the book, we'll make refinement after refinement, starting our focus on the general users of our app, then focusing on power users, and then worrying about other developers helping us with our app, before finally finishing with tools and techniques to help us maintain the app.

## CHAPTER 2

Be Easy to Use

After installing your app, the first experience a user has with it will be the actual command-line interface. If the interface is difficult, counterintuitive, or, well, ugly, it's not going to inspire a lot of confidence, and your users will have a hard time using it to achieve its clear and concise purpose. Conversely, if it's easy to use, your interface will give your application an edge with its audience.

Fortunately, it's easy to get the command-line interface right, once you know the proper tools and techniques. The UNIX command line has a long and storied history, and there are now many conventions and idioms for how to invoke a command-line app. If your app follows these conventions, your users will have an easier time using it. We'll see that even a highly complex app can have a succinct and memorable interface.

In this chapter, we'll learn to use standard library and open source community tools that make it incredibly simple to create a conventional, idiomatic command-line interface whether it's a simple backup script or a complex command-line task management system. We'll learn how to make a simple command-line interface using Ruby's OptionParser class and then tackle a more sophisticated command-suite application, which we'll build using the open source GLI library. But first, we need to get familiar with the proper names of the elements of a typical command-line interface: its options, arguments, and commands.

2.1 Understanding the Command Line: Options, Arguments, and Commands

To tell a command-line application how to do its work, you typically need to enter more than just the name of its executable. For example, we must tell grep which files we want it to search. The database backup app, db_backup.rb, that we introduced in the previous chapter needs a username and password and a database name in order to do its work. The primary way to give an app the information it needs is via *options* and *arguments*, as depicted in Figure 1, *Basic parts of a command-line app invocation*, on page 15. Note that this format isn't imposed by the operating system but is based on the GNU standard for command-line apps.[1] Before we learn how to make a command-line interface that can parse and accept options and arguments, we need to delve a bit deeper into their idioms and conventions. We'll start with options and move on to arguments. After that, we'll discuss *commands*, which are a distinguishing feature of command suites.

Options

Options are the way in which a user modifies the behavior of your app. Consider the two invocations of ls shown here. In the first, we omit options and see the default behavior. In the second, we use the -l option to modify the listing format.

```
$ ls
one.jpg     two.jpg      three.jpg
$ ls -l
-rw-r--r--   1 davec  staff    14005 Jul 13 19:06 one.jpg
-rw-r--r--   1 davec  staff    14005 Jul 11 13:06 two.jpg
-rw-r--r--   1 davec  staff    14005 Jun 10 09:45 three.jpg
```

Options come in two forms: long and short.

Short-form options

> Short-form options are preceded by a dash and are only one character long, for example -l. Short-form options can be combined after a single dash, as in the following example. For example, the following two lines of code produce exactly the same result:

> ls -l -a -t

> ls -lat

Long-form options

> Long-form options are preceded by two dashes and, strictly speaking, consist of two or more characters. However, long-form options are usually complete words (or even several words, separated by dashes). The reason for this is to be explicit about what the option means; with a short-form option, the single letter is often a mnemonic. With long-form options, the convention is to spell the word for what the option does. In the command

---

1. http://www.gnu.org/prep/standards/html_node/Command_002dLine-Interfaces.html

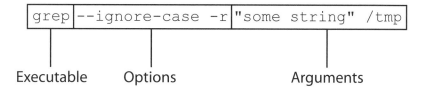

Figure 1—Basic parts of a command-line app invocation

curl --basic http://www.google.com, for example, --basic is a single, long-form option. Unlike short options, long options cannot be combined; each must be entered separately, separated by spaces on the command line.

Command-line options can be one of two types: *switches*, which are used to turn options on and off and do not take arguments, and *flags*, which take arguments, as shown in Figure 2, *A command-line invocation with switches and flags*, on page 16. Flags typically require arguments but, strictly speaking, don't need to do so. They just need to accept them. We'll talk more about this in Chapter 5, *Delight Casual Users*, on page 71.

Typically, if a switch is in the long-form (for example --foo), which turns "on" some behavior, there is also another switch preceded with no- (for example --no-foo) that turns "off" the behavior.

Finally, long-form flags take their argument via an equal sign, whereas in the short form of a flag, an equal sign is typically not used. For example, the curl command, which makes HTTP requests, provides both short-form and long-form flags to specify an HTTP request method: -X and --request, respectively. The following example invocations show how to properly pass arguments to those flags:

curl -X POST http://www.google.com

curl --request=POST http://www.google.com

Although some apps do not require an equal sign between a long-form flag and its argument, your apps should always accept an equal sign, because this is the idiomatic way of giving a flag its argument. We'll see later in this chapter that the tools provided by Ruby and its open source ecosystem make it easy to ensure your app follows this convention.

Arguments

As shown in Figure 1, *Basic parts of a command-line app invocation*, on page 15, arguments are the elements of a command line that aren't options. Rather,

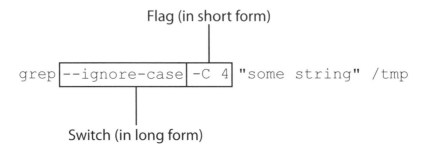

Figure 2—A command-line invocation with switches and flags

arguments represent the objects that the command-line app will operate on. Typically, these objects are file or directory names, but this depends on the app. We might design our database backup app to treat the arguments as the names of the databases to back up.

Not all command-line apps take arguments, while others take an arbitrary number of them. Typically, if your app operates on a file, it's customary to accept any number of filenames as arguments and to operate on them one at a time.

Commands

Figure 1, *Basic parts of a command-line app invocation*, on page 15 shows a diagram of a basic command-line invocation with the main elements of the command line labeled.

For simple command-line applications, options and arguments are all you need to create an interface that users will find easy to use. Some apps, however, are a bit more complicated. Consider git, the popular distributed version control system. git packs a lot of functionality. It can add files to a repository, send them to a remote repository, examine a repository, or fetch changes from another user's repository. Originally, git was packaged as a collection of individual command-line apps. For example, to commit changes, you would execute the git-commit application. To fetch files from a remote repository, you would execute git-fetch. While each command provided its own options and arguments, there was some overlap.

For example, almost every git command provided a --no-pager option, which told git *not* to send output through a pager like more. Under the covers, there was a lot of shared code as well. Eventually, git was repackaged as a single executable that operated as a *command suite*. Instead of running git-commit, you run git commit. The single-purpose command-line app git-commit now becomes a *command* to the new command-suite app, git.

A command in a command-line invocation isn't like an option or an argument; it has a more specific meaning. A command is how you specify the action to take from among a potentially large or complex set of available actions. If you look around the Ruby ecosystem, you'll see that the use of command suites is quite common. gem, rails, and bundler are all types of command suites.

Figure 3, *Basic parts of a command-suite invocation*, on page 18 shows a command-suite invocation, with the command's position on the command line highlighted.

You won't always design your app as a command suite; only if your app is complex enough that different behaviors are warranted will you use this style of interface. Further, if you *do* decide to design your app as a command suite, your app should *require* a command (we'll talk about how your app should behave when the command is omitted in Chapter 3, *Be Helpful*, on page 33).

The command names in your command suite should be short but expressive, with short forms available for commonly used or lengthier commands. For example, Subversion, the version control system used by many developers, accepts the short-form co in place of its checkout command.

A command suite can still accept options; however, their position on the command line affects how they are interpreted.

Global options

> Options that you enter before the command are known as *global options*. Global options affect the global behavior of an app and can be used with any command in the suite. Recall our discussion of the --no-pager option for git? This option affects all of git's commands. We know this because it comes before the command on the command line, as shown in Figure 3, *Basic parts of a command-suite invocation*, on page 18.

Command options

> Options that follow a command are known as *command-specific options* or simply command options. These options have meaning only in the context of their command. Note that they can also have the same names as global options. For example, if our to-do list app took a global option -f to indicate where to find the to-do list's file, the list command might also take an -f to indicate a "full" listing.

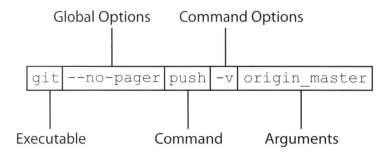

Figure 3—Basic parts of a command-suite invocation

The command-line invocation would be todo -f ~/my_todos.txt list -f. Since the first -f comes before the command and is a global option, we won't confuse it for the second -f, which is a command option.

Most command-line apps follow the conventions we've just discussed. If your app follows them as well, users will have an easier time learning and using your app's interface. For example, if your app accepts long-form flags but doesn't allow the use of an equal sign to separate the flag from its argument, users will be frustrated.

The good news is that it's very easy to create a Ruby app that follows all of the conventions we've discussed in this section. We'll start by enhancing our Chapter 1 database backup app from Chapter 1, *Have a Clear and Concise Purpose*, on page 1 to demonstrate how to make an easy-to-use, conventional command-line application using OptionParser. After that, we'll use GLI to enhance our to-do list app, creating an idiomatic command suite that's easy for our users to use and easy for us to implement.

2.2 Building an Easy-to-Use Command-Line Interface

If you've done a lot of shell scripting (or even written a command-line tool in C), you're probably familiar with getopt,[2] which is a C library for parsing the command line and an obvious choice as a tool for creating your interface. Although Ruby includes a wrapper for getopt, you shouldn't use it, because there's a better built-in option: OptionParser. As you'll see, OptionParser is not only easy to use but is much more sophisticated than getopt and will result in a superior command-line interface for your app. OptionParser code is also easy to read and modify, making enhancements to your app simple to implement.

---

2.   http://en.wikipedia.org/wiki/Getopt

Before we see how to use OptionParser, let's first consider the input our application needs to do its job and the command line that will provide it. We'll use the backup application, db_backup.rb, which we introduced in Chapter 1, *Have a Clear and Concise Purpose*, on page 1. What kind of options might our application need? Right now, it needs the name of a database and some way of knowing when we're doing an "end-of-iteration" backup instead of a normal, daily backup. The app will also need a way to authenticate users of the database server we're backing up; this means a way for the user to provide a username and password.

Since our app will mostly be used for making daily backups, we'll make that its default behavior. This means we can provide a switch to perform an "end-of-iteration" backup. We'll use -i to name the switch, which provides a nice mnemonic (*i* for "iteration"). For the database user and password, -u and -p are obvious choices as flags for the username and password, respectively, as arguments.

To specify the database name, our app could use a flag, for example -d, but the database name actually makes more sense as an argument. The reason is that it really is the object that our backup app operates on. Let's look at a few examples of how users will use our app:

```
$ db_backup.rb small_client
# => does a daily backup of the "small_client" database

$ db_backup.rb -u davec -p P@55WorD medium_client
# => does a daily  backup of the "medium_client" database, using the
#    given username and password to login

$ db_backup.rb -i big_client
# => Do an "end of iteration" backup for the database "big_client"
```

Now that we know what we're aiming for, let's see how to build this interface with OptionParser.

Building a Command-Line Interface with **OptionParser**

To create a simple command-line interface with OptionParser, create an instance of the class and pass it a block. Inside that block, we create the elements of our interface using OptionParser methods. We'll use on to define each option in our command line.

The on itself takes a block, which is called when the user invokes the option it defines. For flags, the block is given the argument the user provided. The simplest thing to do in this block is to simply store the option used into a Hash, storing "true" for switches and the block argument for flags. Once the options are defined, use the parse! method of our instantiated OptionParser class to do the actual command-line parsing. Here's the code to implement the iteration switch and username and password flags of our database application:

```
be_easy_to_use/db_backup/bin/db_backup.rb
#!/usr/bin/env ruby

# Bring OptionParser into the namespace
require 'optparse'

options = {}
option_parser = OptionParser.new do |opts|
  # Create a switch
  opts.on("-i","--iteration") do
    options[:iteration] = true
  end

  # Create a flag
  opts.on("-u USER") do |user|
    options[:user] = user
  end

  opts.on("-p PASSWORD") do |password|
    options[:password] = password
  end
end

option_parser.parse!
puts options.inspect
```

As you can see by inspecting the code, each call to on maps to one of the command-line options we want our app to accept. What's not clear is how OptionParser knows which are switches and which are flags. There is great flexibility in the arguments to on, so the type of the argument, as well as its contents, controls how OptionParser will behave. For example, if a string is passed and it starts with a dash followed by one or more nonspace characters, it's treated as a switch. If there is a space and another string, it's treated as a flag. If multiple option names are given (as we do in the line opts.on("-i","--iteration")), then these two options mean the same thing.

Table 1, *Overview of OptionParser parameters to on*, on page 21 provides an overview of how a parameter to on will be interpreted; you can add as many parameters as you like, in any order. The complete documentation on how these parameters are interpreted is available on the rdoc for the make_switch method.[3]

---

3.   http://www.ruby-doc.org/stdlib/libdoc/optparse/rdoc/files/optparse_rb.html#M001903

Effect	Example	Meaning
Short-form switch	-v	The switch -v is accepted on the command line. Any number of strings like this may appear in the parameter list and will all cause the given block to be called.
Long-form switch	--verbose	The switch --verbose is accepted. Any number of strings like this may appear in the parameter list and can be mixed and matched with the shorter form previously.
Negatable long-form switch	--[no-]verbose	Both --verbose and --no-verbose are accepted. If the no form is used, the block will be passed false; otherwise, true is passed.
Flag with required argument	-n NAME or --name NAME	The option is a *flag*, and it requires an argument. All other option strings provided as parameters will require flags as well (for example, if we added the string --username after the -u USER argument in our code, then --username would also require an argument; we don't need to repeat the USER in the second string). The value provided on the command line is passed to the block.
Flag with optional argument	-n [NAME] or --name [NAME]	The option is a flag whose argument is optional. If the flag's argument is omitted, the block will still be called, but nil will be passed.
Documentation	Any other string	This is a documentation string and will be part of the help output.

Table 1—Overview of **OptionParser** parameters to on

In the blocks given to on, our code simply sets a value in our options hash. Since it's just Ruby code, we can do more than that if we'd like. For example, we could sanity check the options and fail early if the argument to a particular flag were invalid.

Validating Arguments to Flags

Suppose we know that the usernames of all the database users in our systems are of the form first.last. To help our users, we can validate the value of the argument to -u before even connecting to the database. Since the block given to an on method call is invoked whenever a user enters the option it defines, we can check within the block for the presence of a period in the username value, as the following code illustrates:

be_easy_to_use/db_backup/bin/db_backup.rb
```ruby
opts.on("-u USER") do |user|
  unless user =~ /^.+\..+$/
    raise ArgumentError,"USER must be in 'first.last' format"
  end
  options[:user] = user
end
```

Here, we raise an exception if the argument doesn't match our regular expression; this will cause the entire option-parsing process to stop, and our app will exit with the error message we passed to raise.

You can probably imagine that in a complex command-line app, you might end up with a lot of argument validation. Even though it's only a few lines of extra code, it can start to add up. Fortunately, OptionParser is far more flexible than what we've seen so far. The on method is quite sophisticated and can provide a lot of validations for us. For example, we could replace the code we just wrote with the following to achieve the same result:

be_easy_to_use/db_backup/bin/db_backup.rb
```ruby
opts.on("-u USER",
➤        /^.+\..+$/) do |user|
  options[:user] = user
end
```

The presence of a regular expression as an argument to on indicates to OptionParser that it should validate the user-provided argument against this regular expression. Also note that if you include any capturing groups in your regexp (by using parentheses to delineate sections of the regexp), those values will be extracted and passed to the block as an Array. The raw value from the command line will be at index 0, and the extracted values will fill out the rest of the array.

You don't have to use regular expressions for validation, however. By including an Array in the argument list to on, you can indicate the complete list of acceptable values. By using a Hash, OptionParser will use the keys as the acceptable values and send the mapped value to the block, like so:

```
servers = { 'dev' => '127.0.0.1',
            'qa' => 'qa001.example.com',
            'prod' => 'www.example.com' }

opts.on('--server SERVER',servers) do |address|
  # for --server=dev, address would be '127.0.0.1'
  # for --server=prod, address would be 'www.example.com'
end
```

Finally, if you provide a classname in the argument list, OptionParser will attempt to convert the string from the command line into an instance of the given class. For example, if you include the constant Integer in the argument list to on, OptionParser will attempt to parse the flag's argument into an Integer instance for you. There is support for many conversions. See *Type Conversions in OptionParser*, on page 24 for the others available and how to make your own using the accept method.

By using OptionParser, we've written very little code but created an idiomatic UNIX-style interface that will be familiar to anyone using our app. We've seen how to use this to improve our backup app, but how can we create a similarly idiomatic interface for our to-do list app? Our to-do list app is actually a series of commands: "create a new task," "list the tasks," "complete a task." This sounds like a job for the command-suite pattern.

OptionParser works great for a simple app like our backup app; however, it isn't a great fit for parsing the command line of a command suite; it can be done, but it requires jumping through a lot more hoops. Fortunately, several open source libraries are available to make this job easy for us. We'll look at one of them, GLI, in the next section.

2.3 Building an Easy-to-Use Command-Suite Interface

Command suites are more complex by nature than a basic automation or single-purpose command-line app. Since command suites bundle a lot of functionality, it's even more important that they be easy to use. Helping users navigate the commands and their options is crucial.

Let's revisit our to-do list app we discussed in Chapter 1, *Have a Clear and Concise Purpose*, on page 1. We've discussed that the command-suite pattern is the best approach, and we have already identified three commands the app will need: "new," "list," and "done" to create a new task, list the existing tasks, and complete a task, respectively.

We also want our app to provide a way to locate the to-do list file we're operating on. A global option named -f would work well (*f* being a mnemonic for

Type Conversions in OptionParser

While strictly speaking it is not a user-facing feature, OptionParser provides a sophisticated facility for automatically converting flag arguments to a type other than String. The most common conversion is to a number, which can be done by including Integer, Float, or Numeric as an argument to on, like so:

```
ops.on('--verbosity LEVEL',Integer) do |verbosity|
  # verbosity is not a string, but an Integer
end
```

OptionParser provides built-in conversions for the following: Integer, Float, Numeric, DecimalInteger, OctalInteger, DecimalNumeric, FalseClass, and TrueClass. Regexp support is provided, and it looks for a string starting and ending with a slash (/), for example --matches "/^bar/". OptionParser will also parse an Array, treating each comma as an item delimiter; for example, --items "foo,bar,blah" yields the list ["foo","bar","blah"].

You can write your own conversions as well, by passing the object and a block to the accept method on an OptionParser. The object is what you'd also pass to on to trigger the conversion (typically it would be a class). The block takes a string argument and returns the converted type.

You could use it to convert a string into a Hash like so:

```
opts.accept(Hash) do |string|
  hash = {}
  string.split(',').each do |pair|
    key,value = pair.split(/:/)
    hash[key] = value
  end
  hash
end

opts.on('--custom ATTRS',Hash) do |hash|
  custom_attributes = hash
end
```

A command like foo --custom foo:bar,baz:quux will result in custom_attributes getting the value { 'foo' => 'bar', 'baz' => 'quux' }.

Automatic conversions like these can be very handy for complex applications.

"file"). It would be handy if our "new" command allowed us to set a priority or place a new task directly at the top of our list. -p is a good name for a flag that accepts a priority as an argument, and we'll use -f to name a switch that means "first in the list."

We'll allow our list command to take a sort option, so it will need a flag named -s. done won't need any special flags right now. Let's see a few examples of the interface we want to create:

```
$ todo new "Rake leaves"
# => Creates a new todo in the default location

$ todo -f /home/davec/work.txt new "Refactor database"
# => Creates a new todo in /home/davec/work.txt instead
#    of the default

$ todo -f /home/davec/work.txt new "Do design review" -f
# => Create the task "Do design review" as the first
#    task in our task list in /home/davec/work.txt

$ todo list -s name
# => List all of our todos, sorted by name

$ todo done 3
# => Complete task #3
```

Unfortunately, OptionParser was not built with command suites in mind, and we can't directly use it to create this sort of interface. To understand why, look at our third invocation of the new command: both the "filename" global flag and the command-specific "first" switch have the same name: -f. If we ask OptionParser to parse that command line, we won't be able to tell which -f is which.

A command-line interface like this is too complex to do "by hand." What we need is a tool custom-built for parsing the command line of a command suite.

Building a Command Suite with GLI

Fortunately, many open source tools are available to help us parse the command-suite interface we've designed for our to-do list app. Three common ones are commander,[4] thor,[5] and GLI.[6] They are all quite capable, but we're going to use GLI here. GLI is actively maintained, has extensive documentation, and was special-built for making command-suite apps very easily (not to mention written by the author of this book). Its syntax is similar to commander and thor, with all three being inspired by rake; therefore, much of what we'll learn here is applicable to the other libraries (we'll see how to use them in a bit more depth in Appendix 1, *Common Command-Line Gems and Libraries*, on page 175).

---

4. http://visionmedia.github.com/commander/
5. https://github.com/wycats/thor
6. https://github.com/davetron5000/gli

Rather than modify our existing app with GLI library calls, we'll take advantage of a feature of GLI called *scaffolding*. We'll use it to bootstrap our app's UI and show us immediately how to declare our user interface.

Building a Skeleton App with GLI's scaffold

Once we install GLI, we can use it to bootstrap our app. The gli application is itself a command suite, and we'll use the scaffold command to get started. gli scaffold takes an arbitrary number of arguments, each representing a command for our new command suite. You don't have to think of all your commands up front. Adding them later is simple, but for now, as the following console session shows, it's easy to set up the commands you know you will need. For our to-do app, these include new, list, and done.

```
$ gem install gli
Successfully installed gli-1.3.0
1 gem installed
$ gli scaffold to-do new list done
Creating dir ./todo/lib...
Creating dir ./todo/bin...
Creating dir ./todo/test...
Created ./todo/bin/todo
Created ./todo/README.rdoc
Created ./todo/todo.rdoc
Created ./todo/todo.gemspec
Created ./todo/test/tc_nothing.rb
Created ./todo/Rakefile
Created ./todo/Gemfile
Created ./todo/lib/todo_version.rb
```

Don't worry about all those files that scaffold creates just yet; we'll explain them in future chapters. Now, let's test the new interface before we look more closely at the code:

```
$ bin/todo new
$ bin/todo done
$ bin/todo list
$ bin/todo foo
error: Unknown command 'foo'. Use 'todo help' for a list of commands
```

As you can see from the session dialog, our scaffolded app recognizes our commands, even though they're not yet implemented. We even get an error when we try to use the command foo, which we didn't declare. Let's now look at the code GLI produces to see how it works. Note that GLI has generated only the code it needs to parse the commands we passed as arguments to the scaffold command. The switches and flags GLI sets up are merely examples; we'll see how to customize them later.

We'll go through the generated code step by step. First, we need to set up our app to bring GLI's libraries in, via a require and an include.

be_easy_to_use/todo/bin/todo
```ruby
#!/usr/bin/env ruby

require 'rubygems'
require 'gli'
include GLI
```

Since we've included GLI, the remaining code is mostly method calls from the GLI module.[7] The next thing the code does is to declare some global options.

be_easy_to_use/todo/bin/todo
```ruby
switch :s
flag   :f
```

This declares that the app accepts a global switch -s and a global flag -f. Remember, these are just examples; we'll change them later to meet our app's requirements. Next, the code defines the new command:

be_easy_to_use/todo/bin/todo
```ruby
command :new do |c|

  c.switch :s
  c.flag :f

  c.action do |global_options,options,args|
    # Your command logic here

    # If you have any errors, just raise them
    # raise "that command made no sense"
  end
end
```

The block given to command establishes a context to declare command-specific options via the argument passed to the block (c). GLI has provided an example of command-specific options by declaring that the new command accepts a switch -s and a flag -f. Finally, we call the action method on c and give it a block. This block will be executed when the user executes the new command and is where we'd put the code to implement new. The block will be given the parsed global options, the parsed command-specific options, and the command-line arguments via global_options, options, and args, respectively.

GLI has generated similar code for the other commands we specified to gli scaffold:

---

7.   http://davetron5000.github.com/gli/classes/GLI.html

```
be_easy_to_use/todo/bin/todo
command :list do |c|
  c.action do |global_options,options,args|
  end
end

command :done do |c|
  c.action do |global_options,options,args|
  end
end
```

The last step is to ask GLI to parse the command line and run our app. The run method returns with an appropriate exit code for our app (we'll learn all about exit codes in Chapter 4, *Play Well with Others*, on page 53).

```
be_easy_to_use/todo/bin/todo
exit GLI.run(ARGV)
```

GLI has provided us with a skeleton app that parses the command line for us; all we have to do is fill in the code (and replace GLI's example options with our own).

Turning the Scaffold into an App

As we discussed previously, we need a global way to specify the location of the to-do list file, and we need our new command to take a flag to specify the position of a new task, as well as a switch to specify "this task should go first." The list command needs a flag to control the way tasks are sorted.

Here's the GLI code to make this interface. We've also added some simple debugging, so when we run our app, we can see that the command line is properly parsed.

```
be_easy_to_use/todo/bin/todo_integrated.rb
➤ flag :f
➤
  command :new do |c|

➤   c.flag :priority
➤   c.switch :f

    c.action do |global_options,options,args|
      puts "Global:"
      puts "-f - #{global_options[:f]}"
      puts "Command:"
      puts "-f - #{options[:f] ? 'true' : 'false'}"
      puts "-p - #{options[:p]}"
      puts "args - #{args.join(',')}"
    end
  end
```

```
command :list do |c|
```
➤
```
  c.flag :s
```
➤
```
  c.action do |global_options,options,args|
    puts "Global:"
    puts "-f - #{global_options[:f]}"
    puts "Command:"
    puts "-s - #{options[:s]}"
  end
end

command :done do |c|
  c.action do |global_options,options,args|
    puts "Global:"
    puts "-f - #{global_options[:f]}"
  end
end
```

The highlighted code represents the changes we made to what GLI generated. We've removed the example global and command-specific options and replaced them with our own. Note that we can use both short-form and long-form options; GLI knows that a single-character symbol like :f is a short-form option but a multicharacter symbol like :priority is a long-form option. We also added some calls to puts that demonstrate how we access the parsed command line (in lieu of the actual logic of our to-do list app). Let's see it in action:

```
$ bin/todo -f ~/todo.txt new -f "A new task" "Another task"
Global:
-f - /Users/davec/todo.txt
Command:
-f - true
-p -
args - A new task,Another task
```

We can see that :f in global_options contains the file specified on the command line; that options[:f] is true, because we used the command-specific option -f; and that options[:priority] is missing, since we didn't specify that on the command line at all.

Once we've done this, we can add our business logic to each of the c.action blocks, using global_options, options, and args as appropriate. For example, here's how we might implement the logic for the to-do app list command:

```
c.action do |global_options,options,args|
  todos = read_todos(global_options[:filename])
  if options[:s] == 'name'
    todos = todos.sort { |a,b| a <=> b }
  end
```

```
todos.each do |todo|
  puts todo
end
end
```

We've used very few lines of code yet can parse a sophisticated user interface. It's a UI that users will find familiar, based on their past experience with other command suites. It also means that when we add more features to our app, it'll be very simple.

Is there anything else that would be helpful to the user on the command line? Other than some help documentation (which we'll develop in the next chapter), it would be nice if users could use the tab-completion features of their shell to help complete the commands of our command suite. Although our to-do app has only three commands now, it might need more later, and tab completion is a big command-line usability win.

Adding Tab Completion with GLI help and bash

An advantage of defining our command-suite's user interface in the declarative style supported by GLI is that the result provides us with a model of our UI that we can use to do more than simply parse the command line. We can use this model, along with the sophisticated completion function of bash, to let the user tab-complete our suite's commands. First we tell bash that we want special completion for our app, by adding this to our ~/.bashrc and restarting our shell session:

```
complete -F get_todo_commands todo
```

The complete command tells bash to run a function (in our case, get_todo_commands) whenever a user types the command (in our case, todo) followed by a space and some text (optionally) and then hits the a Tab key (i.e., is asked to complete something). complete expects the function to return the possible matches in the shell variable COMPREPLY, as shown in the implementation of get_todo_commands (which also goes in our .bashrc):

```
function get_todo_commands()
{
    if [ -z $2 ] ; then
        COMPREPLY=(`todo help -c`)
    else
        COMPREPLY=(`todo help -c $2`)
    fi
}
```

Every GLI-powered app includes a built-in command called help that is mostly used for getting online help (we'll see more about this in the next chapter).

This command also takes a switch and an optional argument you can use to facilitate tab completion.

The switch -c tells help to output the app's commands in a format suitable for bash completion. If the argument is also provided, the app will list only those commands that match the argument. Since our bash function is given an optional second argument representing what the user has entered thus far on the command line, we can use that to pass to help.

The end result is that your users can use tab completion with your app, and the chance of entering a nonexistent command is now very minimal—all without having to lift a finger! Note that for this to work, you must have todo installed in your PATH (we'll see how users can do this in Chapter 7, *Distribute Painlessly*, on page 101).

```
$ todo help -c
done
help
list
new
$ todo <TAB>
done help list new
$ todo d<TAB>
$ todo done
```

2.4 Moving On

We've learned in this chapter how simple it is to make an easy-to-use interface for a command-line application using built-in or open source libraries. With tools like OptionParser and GLI, you can spend more time on your app and rest easy knowing your user interface will be top notch and highly usable, even as you add new and more complex features.

Now that we know how to easily design and parse a good command-line interface, we need to find a way to let the user know how it works. In the next chapter, we'll talk about in-app help, specifically how OptionParser and GLI make it easy to create and format help text, as well as some slightly philosophical points about what makes good command-line help.

## CHAPTER 3

Be Helpful

In the previous chapter, we learned how to make an easy-to-use command-line interface. We learned the elements that make a well-formed command-line interface and how to design simple apps and command suites that accept arguments, flags, switches, and commands in an unsurprising[1] way. What we didn't talk about was how a user finds out what options and commands such apps provide, what their options mean, and what arguments they accept or require. Without this information, our app might do the job expected of it, but it won't be very helpful.

Fortunately for us, the standard Ruby library OptionParser and the open source GLI gem give us the power to make our app helpful without a lot of effort. In fact, you'll see that it's actually *harder* to make an unhelpful app using these tools. We'll begin by exploring how you can add help and documentation to the pair of apps—db_backup.rb and todo—whose UI we developed in the previous chapter. We'll also look at ways to create more detailed user documentation with an open source library that can bundle UNIX-style manual pages with our app. We'll end the chapter with a look at some rules of thumb for making our documentation useful to both new users of our software and seasoned veterans.

3.1 Documenting a Command-Line Interface

An experienced command-line user will try one or two things on the command line to discover how to use an app: they will run it without arguments or give it a help switch, such as -h or --help (-help is also a possibility because many X-Windows apps respond to this for help). In each case, the user will expect

---

to see a one-screen summary of the app's usage, including what arguments the app accepts or requires and what options are available.

Because db_backup.rb uses OptionParser, we're most of the way there already. Apps that use OptionParser respond to -h and --help in just the way our users expect. When OptionParser encounters either of these switches on the command line (assuming you haven't overridden them), it will display basic help text that shows how to invoke the app and what options it accepts. Here's what OptionParser displays when a user enters an -h or --help option for db_backup.rb:

```
$ db_backup.rb -h
Usage: db_backup [options]
    -i, --iteration
    -u USER
    -p PASSWORD
$ db_backup.rb --help
Usage: db_backup [options]
    -i, --iteration
    -u USER
    -p PASSWORD
```

While OptionParser nicely formats the help screen for us, what's still missing is documentation to explain the meaning of each option. Even though the flags are somewhat self-documenting (e.g., a user will likely figure out that "PASSWORD" is the database password), they still bear further explanation. For example, because usernames are required to be in a certain format, the app should let users know that. The app also requires an argument—the name of the database to back up—and this should be documented in the help text as well.

Documenting Command-Line Options

Once we fill in the documentation, we'd like our help text to look like so:

```
$ db_backup.rb --help
Usage: db_backup [options]
    -i, --iteration   Indicate that this backup is an "iteration" backup
    -u USER           Database username, in first.last format
    -p PASSWORD       Database password
```

Now the user can see exactly what the options mean and what constraints are placed on them (e.g., the username's format). Achieving this with Option-Parser couldn't be simpler. If you recall from Table 1, *Overview of OptionParser parameters to on*, on page 21, any string given as a parameter to on that doesn't match the format of an option will be treated as documentation. So, all we need to do is add some strings to the end of our argument list to each of calls to on:

be_helpful/db_backup/bin/db_backup.rb

```
opts.on('-i','--iteration',
➤       'Indicate that this backup is an "iteration" backup') do
  options[:iteration] = true
end
opts.on('-u USER',
➤       'Database username, in first.last format',
        /^[^.]+\.[^.]+$/) do |user|
  options[:user] = user
end

opts.on('-p PASSWORD',
➤       'Database password') do |password|
  options[:password] = password
end
```

That's all there is too it—not bad for about thirty seconds of coding! Next, we need to document that our app takes the name of the database to back up as an argument.

Documenting Command-Line Arguments

OptionParser provides no way to explicitly document the arguments that a command-line app accepts or requires. You'll note that OptionParser does, however, display an invocation template as its first line of help text (Usage: db_backup.rb [options]). This is called the *banner* and is the perfect place to document our app's arguments. We'd like to append a description of our app's argument to OptionParser's banner so that our help screen looks like so:

```
$ bin/db_backup.rb -h
➤ Usage: db_backup.rb [options] database_name

    -i, --iteration   Indicate that this backup is an "iteration" backup
    -u USER           Database username, in first.last format
    -p PASSWORD       Database password
```

Did you notice that the string database_name now appears in the highlighted line? This is just enough information to tell the user that we require an argument and that it should be the name of the database. OptionParser has a property, banner, that we can set to accomplish this. Since our app currently doesn't set the banner, we get the default that we saw previously. Unfortunately, we cannot directly access this string and tack on database_name, so we'll have to re-create it ourselves.

The other tricky bit is that we don't want to hard-code the name of our app in the banner. If we did, we'd have to update our documentation if we chose to rename our app.

Fortunately, Ruby provides an answer. When an app runs, Ruby sets the global variable $PROGRAM_NAME to the full path name of the app's *executable*, which is the name of the physical file on disk that the operating system uses to run our app. The filename (without the full path) is the name of our app and what the user will type on the command line to run it, so we want to show only that.

Ruby's File class has a handy method named basename that will give us just the name of the file of our executable, without the path to it, which is exactly what we need to create our banner.

```
be_helpful/db_backup/bin/db_backup.rb
option_parser = OptionParser.new do |opts|
  executable_name = File.basename($PROGRAM_NAME)
  opts.banner = "Usage: #{executable_name} [options] database_name"
```

Now the user can easily see that our app requires one argument: the name of the database to back up. Note that we are using an underscore notation here; if we had written "database name" instead (using a space between the two words), a user might misinterpret the words as calling for two arguments, one called "database" and another called "name."

It's hard to think of adding one string to our app's help text as "documentation," but for apps as straightforward as ours, this is sufficient. The user knows that db_backup.rb backs up a database, and the string database_name is all the user needs in order to know that our argument is the name of the database to back up. Some apps have more complex arguments, and we'll see later how we can bundle more detailed documentation with our app to explain them.

The last thing we need to do is to provide a brief summary of the purpose of our app so that occasional users can get a quick reminder of what it does.

Adding a Brief Description for a Command-Line Application

A user who has just installed our app will certainly remember its purpose, but someone running it weeks or months from now might not. Although it's not hard to guess that an app named db_backup backs up a database, occasional users might not recall that it's only for backing up MySQL databases and won't work on, say, an Oracle database. To be helpful to these users, db_backup.rb --help should include a brief summary of the app's purpose. This should be the first thing the user sees when asking for help, like so:

```
$ bin/db_backup.rb -h
```
➤ Backup one or more MySQL databases

Usage: db_backup.rb [options] database_name

```
    -i, --iteration    Indicate that this backup is an "iteration" backup
    -u USER            Database username, in first.last format
    -p PASSWORD        Database password
```

Like the usage statement, OptionParser doesn't provide a place to explicitly document our app's purpose, but we can add it to the banner, just like we did when we documented its arguments. Since the banner is going to be multiline, we can format it directly in our source using multiple lines (instead of putting control characters like \n in a single-line string) so that the banner text is easy to read and modify:

be_helpful/db_backup/bin/db_backup.rb
```
option_parser = OptionParser.new do |opts|
  executable_name = File.basename($PROGRAM_NAME)
  opts.banner = "Backup one or more MySQL databases

Usage: #{executable_name} [options] database_name

"
```

You might be tempted to add more documentation to the banner, but this is not what the banner is for. The banner should be brief and to the point, designed as reference. We'll see later in this chapter how we can provide more detailed help and examples.

Now that we've fully documented what our app does, how to invoke it, and what options are available, db_backup.rb seems pretty darn helpful. There's only one thing left to consider: what if the user executes db_backup.rb but omits the required argument, the database name?

We mentioned earlier that experienced command-line users might do this on purpose, as a way to get a help statement. The user could also do this by accident, forgetting to provide a database name. No matter what the user's intent might be, our app behaves the same: unhelpfully. It will likely generate an exception or, worse, fail silently.

In cases like this, where you don't know whether the user made a mistake or is just looking for help, you should cover both bases and provide an error message, followed by the help text. Let's see how to do this by looking at db_backup.rb.

Ruby places all command-line arguments in an array called ARGV, which OptionParser modifies when parse! is called. OptionParser's modification to ARGV is to remove all the options and arguments it knows about. What's left in ARGV are the unparsed arguments, which you can safely treat as the arguments the user provided on the command line. Unrecognized *switches and flags* will cause OptionParser to print an error and exit your app, so you'll never find them in ARGV.

All we need to do to detect this "request for help or erroneous invocation" situation is check that ARGV is empty *after* having OptionParser parse the command line, as shown in the following code:

be_helpful/db_backup/bin/db_backup.rb
```
option_parser.parse!
➤ if ARGV.empty?
    puts "error: you must supply a database_name"
    puts
    puts option_parser.help
  else
    database_name = ARGV[0]
    # proceed as normal to backup database_name
  end
```

Now db_backup.rb is as helpful as it can be:

```
$ db_backup.rb
➤ error: you must supply a database name

Backup one or more MySQL databases

Usage: db_backup.rb [options] database_name

    -i, --iteration  Indicate that this backup is an "iteration" backup
    -u USER          Database username, in first.last format
    -p PASSWORD      Database password
```

We've seen how easy it is to make a helpful user interface for simple command-line apps using OptionParser, but what about command suites? It's doubly important to provide a helpful user interface, because a command suite is naturally more complex. In the next section, we'll see how to do that by enhancing our to-do list app todo.

3.2 Documenting a Command Suite

Since command suites like todo are more complex than simpler command-line apps like db_backup.rb, it's important that we have documentation and that it's easy to access. Users need to know not only what each option does and what the arguments mean but also what commands are available and what they do. The best way to provide this information is via a two-level help system. At the top "level," we see the "banner"-type information, the global options, the list of commands, and what each command does. This information should be provided when the app is invoked with no arguments or when invoked with the command help, like so:

```
$ bin/todo help
usage: todo [global options] command [command options]

Version: 0.0.1

Global Options:
    -f, --filename=todo_file - Path to the todo file (default: ~/.todo.txt)

Commands:
    done - Complete a task
    help - Shows list of commands or help for one command
    list - List tasks
    new  - Create a new task in the task list
```

The second "level" is where help on a particular command is displayed. This type of help can include more detail about what the command does and should also document the command-specific options and arguments. Users should be able to access this using the command-suite's help command, giving the command name as an argument, like so:

```
$ bin/todo help new
new [command options] task_name
    Create a new task in the task list

    A task has a name and a priority. By default, new tasks
    have the lowest possible priority, though this can be
    overridden.

Command Options:
    -f          - put the new task first in the list
    -p priority - set the priority of the new task, 1 being the highest
```

This may sound complex; however, open source libraries like GLI actually make this quite simple. Apps that use GLI, like todo, include a help command by default, which provides the two-level help system we just described. We can see this in action by running our todo app right now:

```
$ bin/todo help
usage: todo [global options] command [command options]

Version: 0.0.1
```

```
Global Options:
    -f, --filename=arg -

Commands:
    done -
    help - Shows list of commands or help for one command
    list -
    new  -
```
$ **bin/todo help new**
```
new
```

Like OptionParser, GLI provides the scaffolding and support for the help system and even formats everything for us; we just need to provide the help text for the global options, the commands, their options, and their arguments. This is done in GLI via three methods:

desc   Provides a short, one-line summary of a command or option

long_desc Provides a more detailed explanation of a command or option (later, we'll talk about the difference between this and the shorter summary you'd put in desc)

arg_name Gives the argument to a command or flag a short, descriptive name

Once we fill in our app using these methods, our help system will look just like the one shown at the start of this section. Here's what the new command's implementation looks like when fully documented using these methods:

be_helpful/todo/bin/todo
```
➤ desc 'Create a new task in the task list'
➤ long_desc """
➤ A task has a name and a priority. By default, new
➤ tasks have the lowest possible priority, though
➤ this can be overridden.
➤ """
➤ arg_name 'task_name'
  command :new do |c|

➤   c.desc 'set the priority of the new task, 1 being the highest'
➤   c.arg_name 'priority'
    c.flag :p

➤   c.desc 'put the new task first in the list'
    c.switch :f

    c.action do |global_options,options,args|
    end
  end
```

As you can see, we call desc, long_desc, and arg_name *before* the element they document. This is exactly how Rake works (and also how we document our code; documentation comments appear before the code they document). This keeps our app's code very readable and maintainable.

Now that we've filled this in, our app comes alive with an easy-to-use help system:

```
$ bin/todo help
usage: todo [global options] command [command options]

Version: 0.0.1

Global Options:
    -f, --filename=todo_file - Path to the todo file (default: ~/.todo.txt)

Commands:
    done - Complete a task
    help - Shows list of commands or help for one command
    list - List tasks
    new  - Create a new task in the task list

$ bin/todo help new
new [command options] task_name
    Create a new task in the task list

    A task has a name and a priority. By default, new tasks
    have the lowest possible priority, though this can be
    overridden.

Command Options:
    -f           - put the new task first in the list
    -p priority - set the priority of the new task, 1 being the highest
```

One last thing that's worth pointing out is the documentation for the global flag, -f. You'll note that our documentation string includes (default: ~/.todo.txt). We didn't include that in the string given to desc; it's an additional bit of documentation the GLI derives for us when we use the default_value method to indicate the default value for a flag.

```
be_helpful/todo/bin/todo
desc "Path to the todo file"
arg_name "todo_file"
➤ default_value "~/.todo.txt"
flag :f
```

default_value isn't actually for documentation; it allows us to specify the value for a flag when the user omits it from the command line; this means that the value of global_options[:f] will not be nil; it will be ~/.todo.txt if the user omits -f on the command line. GLI helpfully includes this in our help text, meaning our documentation and our code will always be consistent.

We've now learned how easy it is to provide help documentation for simple command-line apps and command suites. By adding a few extra strings to our code, our apps can easily help users understand what the apps do and how to use them. But not all apps are so simple. Command-line apps often provide sophisticated behavior that can't be easily explained in the one or two lines of text available in the built-in help systems. How can we provide detailed documentation beyond simple help text?

3.3   Including a Man Page

As we've seen, it's easy to document the options, arguments, and commands of a command-line app. This information, and the ability to access it from the app itself, is invaluable to repeat users of your app; they can quickly find out how to use your app the way they need to get their work done. What if we need more? Perhaps we'd like some longer examples for new users, or perhaps our app is sufficiently complex that we need more space to explain things.

Even a straightforward app like db_backup.rb can benefit from a few examples and some detailed documentation (such as an explanation of the "iteration backup" concept or why the username must be in first.last format). There isn't enough space in the built-in help provided by OptionParser for this information. Furthermore, these are not details that a regular user will need. Frequent users will just want the usage statement and options reference via --help and won't need tutorials, examples, or detailed documentation when they just need to get a list of options.

A traditional UNIX app provides this detailed information in a *manual*, or *man*, page, which users access via the man command. If you type man ls on the command line, you'll see a nice, detailed explanation of the ls command. However, although you could bundle a man page with your Ruby command-line app, man wouldn't be able to access it easily because of the way RubyGems installs apps (we'll talk more about RubyGems in Chapter 7, *Distribute Painlessly*, on page 101). Even if man *could* access your app's files, creating a man page is no small feat; it requires using the nroff[2] format, which is cumbersome to use for writing documentation.

---

2.   http://en.wikipedia.org/wiki/Nroff

Fortunately, the Ruby ecosystem of open source libraries has us covered. gem-man,[3] a plug-in to RubyGems created by GitHub's Chris Wanstrath, allows users to access man pages bundled inside a gem via the gem man command. ronn[4] is a Ruby app that allows us to create man pages in plain text, without having to learn nroff. We can use these two tools together to create a manual page that we can easily distribute with our app and that will be easily accessible to our users.

Once we've installed these tools, created our man page, and distributed our app to users, they'll be able to read whatever detailed documentation we've provided like so:

```
$ gem man db_backup
DB_BACKUP.RB(1)                              DB_BACKUP.RB(1)


NAME
      db_backup.rb - backup one or more MySQL databases

SYNOPSIS
      db_backup.rb database_name
      db_backup.rb -u username -p password database_name
      db_backup.rb -i|--iteration database_name
etc....
```

Installing Man Page Tools

Installing gem-man and ronn is straightforward using RubyGems' gem command:

```
$ gem install gem-man ronn
Successfully installed gem-man-0.2.0
Building native extensions.  This could take a while...
Building native extensions.  This could take a while...
Successfully installed hpricot-0.8.4
Successfully installed rdiscount-1.6.8
Successfully installed mustache-0.99.4
Successfully installed ronn-0.7.3
5 gems installed
```

The extra gems installed are gems needed by ronn (we'll talk about runtime dependencies later in Chapter 7, *Distribute Painlessly*, on page 101).

Now that we have our libraries and tools installed, we need to set up a location for our man page's source to live in our project. By convention, this location is a directory called man, and our source file is named APP_NAME.1.ronn (where APP_NAME is the name of our app).

---

3.   http://defunkt.io/gem-man/
4.   http://rtomayko.github.com/ronn/

```
$ mkdir man
$ touch man/db_backup.1.ronn
```

Although the directory man is just a convention, the .1 in our filename is required. This number represents the "section" of the manual where our man page will live. The UNIX manual has several sections, and section 1 is for command-line executables.[5] The other part of the name (db_backup) is the name users will use to read our app's manual page. Technically we could call it something else, like foobar, but then our users would need to run gem man foobar instead of gem man db_backup. So, we use the name of our app as the base of the filename.

Now that we have all the pieces in place, let's create our man page.

Creating a Man Page with ronn

We said earlier that ronn allows us to write a man page in plain text, without having to use nroff. This is only partially true. What ronn really does is allow us to use the plain-text format Markdown[6] to write our man page. Markdown text looks like plain text but actually follows some lightweight conventions for formatting lists, calling out sections, and creating hyperlinks. It's much simpler than HTML and a lot easier to create than nroff. The ronn-format documentation[7] provides a comprehensive reference for the Markdown syntax relevant to a man page. Text formatted in Markdown is actually quite simple, so let's take a look at some. Here's what a man page for db_backup.rb looks like:

be_helpful/db_backup/man/db_backup.1.ronn
```
db_backup.rb(1) -- backup one or more MySQL databases
======================================================

## SYNOPSIS

`db_backup.rb` <database_name><br>
`db_backup.rb` `-u username` `-p password` <database_name><br>
`db_backup.rb` `-i`|`--iteration` <database_name>

## DESCRIPTION

**db_backup.rb** is a simple command-line tool for backing up a
MySQL database.  It does so safely and quietly, using a sensible
name for the backup files, so it's perfect for use with cron as
a daily backup.
```

---

5. The Wikipedia entry for the UNIX man system (http://en.wikipedia.org/wiki/Man_page#Manual_sections) has a good overview of the other sections if you are interested.

6. http://daringfireball.net/projects/markdown/

7. http://rtomayko.github.com/ronn/ronn-format.7.html

My default, `db_backup.rb` makes a daily backup and names the resulting backup file with the date. `db_backup.rb` also understands our development process, so if you specify the `--iteration` flag, the backup will be named differently than for a daily backup. This will allow you to easily keep one backup per iteration, easily identifying it, and differentiate it from daily backups.

By default, `db_backup.rb` will use your database credentials in `~/.my.cnf`, however, you can override either the username or password (or both) via the `-u` and `-p` flags, respectively.

Finally, `db_backup.rb` will add a sanity check on your username, to make sure it fits with our corporate standard format of `first.last`.

FILES

`~/.my.cnf` is used for authentication if `-u` or `-p` is omitted.

OPTIONS

  * `-i`, `--iteration`:
    Indicate that this backup is an "end of iteration" backup.
  * `-u USER`:
    Database username, in first.last format
    `~/my.cnf` is not correct
  * `-p PASSWORD`:
    Database password

EXAMPLES

Backup the database "big_client"

    $ db_backup.rb big_client

Backup the database "small_client", for which different credentials are required:

    $ db_backup.rb -u dave -p d4v3 small_client

Make an iteration backup of the "big_client" database:

    $ db_backup.rb -i big_client

The formatting reads very well just as plain text, but the Markdown format tells ronn things like this:

- ## marks the beginning of a new section.
- A string like **db_backup.rb** should be displayed in bold.
- Paragraphs preceded by asterisks are a bullet list.

Content-wise, we've replicated some of the information from our code to OptionParser, and we've expanded on a few topics so that a newcomer has a lot more information about how things work. We've also taken advantage of the standard sections that might appear in a man page so that experienced users can quickly jump to the section they are interested in. We'll talk about what sections you might want to include on a man page in the final part of this chapter.

To actually generate our man page from the Markdown source, we use ronn as follows:

```
$ ronn man/db_backup.1.ronn
    roff: man/db_backup.1
    html: man/db_backup.1.html
```

ronn also generates an HTML version suitable for including on your app's website. To preview our man page as command-line users will see it, we can use the UNIX man command on the nroff file generated by ronn:

```
$ man man/db_backup.1
DB_BACKUP.RB(1)                          DB_BACKUP.RB(1)

NAME
       db_backup.rb - backup one or more MySQL databases

SYNOPSIS
       db_backup.rb database_name
       db_backup.rb -u username -p password database_name
       db_backup.rb -i|--iteration database_name
```

We've omitted most of the man page content for brevity, but you can see that it's nicely formatted like any other UNIX man page. To have this man page distributed with our app, we'll need to learn more about RubyGems, which we'll do later in Chapter 7, *Distribute Painlessly*, on page 101. For now, we'll just tell you that if you include this file in your gem and another user installs your app via RubyGems, users will be able to read your man page right from the command line.[8]

```
$ gem man db_backup
DB_BACKUP.RB(1)                          DB_BACKUP.RB(1)

NAME
       db_backup.rb - backup one or more MySQL databases
```

---

8. Savvy users can alias man to be gem man -s, which tells gem-man to use the system manual for any command it doesn't know, thus providing one unified interface to the system manual and the manual of installed Ruby command-line apps.

```
SYNOPSIS
     db_backup.rb database_name
     db_backup.rb -u username -p password database_name
     db_backup.rb -i|--iteration database_name
```

This, combined with the great built-in help that OptionParser or GLI gives you, will ensure that your app is helpful to all users, allowing them to easily and quickly understand how to use your app. You'll be free to focus on what your app does instead of formatting and maintaining documentation.

We now know the nuts and bolts of creating help and documentation, but it's worth having a brief discussion on style. There remain a few aspects of help that are "fuzzy" but nevertheless important, and knowledge of a few more documentation conventions will help you write great documentation without being too verbose.

3.4 Writing Good Help Text and Documentation

That your app has any help text at all is great and puts it, sadly, ahead of many apps in terms of ease of use and user friendliness. We don't want to be merely great; we want to be awesome, so it's important that our help text and documentation be clear, concise, accurate, and useful. We're not going to get into the theory of written communication, but there are a few rules of thumb, as well as some formatting conventions, that will help elevate our help text and documentation.

In general, your in-app help documentation should serve as a concise reference. The only portion of the in-app help that needs to be instructive to a newcomer is the "banner," that is, the one-sentence description of your program. Everything else should be geared toward allowing regular users of your program to remember what options there are and what they do.

Anything else should go into your man page and should include information useful to a newcomers (particularly the "DESCRIPTION" and "EXAMPLE" sections), examples, and more in-depth information for advanced users who want to dig deeper.

Let's walk through each element of our app's documentation and discuss how best to write it.

Documenting an App's Description and Invocation Syntax

The first thing a user will expect to see is the banner, which, in the case of db_backup.rb, contains a one-line description of the app, along with its invocation syntax. This description should be one *very* short sentence that sums up what the app does. If it's longer than sixty characters, it's probably too long, and you should try to summarize it better. (The number sixty is based on a standard terminal width of eighty characters; the difference of twenty characters gives you plenty of breathing room for the name of the app and some whitespace, but in general it forces you to be concise, which is a good thing.)

The invocation syntax or "usage" should follow a fairly strict format. For non-command-suite apps, it will be as follows:

«*executable*» [options] «*arg_name1*» «*arg_name2*»

where *«executable»* is the name of your executable and *«arg_name1»* and *«arg _name2»* are the names of your arguments. Note that [options] should be included only if your app takes options; omit it if it doesn't.

For a command suite, the format is very similar; however, you need to account for the placement of the command and the differentiation of global and command-specific options. GLI's behavior here is what you want:

«*executable*» [global options] «*command*» [command options] «*arg_name1*» «*arg_name2*»

Here, *«command»* is the command being executed. Much like a simple command-line app, you should omit [global options] if your command suite doesn't take global options and omit [command options] if the particular command doesn't take command-specific options.

In other cases, the arguments' names should be brief, with multiple words separated by underscores. If your app requires a lot of arguments, this may be an indicator that you have not designed your UI humanely; you should consider turning those arguments into flags.

If your app takes multiple arguments of the same type (such as a list of files on which to operate), use an ellipsis, like so: arg_name.... The ellipsis is a common indicator that one or more arguments of the same type may be passed, so, in the case of our database backup app, since we accept multiple database names, we should use database_name... to indicate this.

You also might be wondering why the options are documented using square brackets. This is because options are optional, and the UNIX convention is to show optional elements in square brackets. If you recall from Table 1, *Overview of OptionParser parameters to on*, on page 21, a string like "-n [NAME]" indicates to OptionParser that the argument NAME to the flag -n is optional. The reason OptionParser uses square brackets is because of this convention.

It might be possible that your app requires certain options to always be set on the command line; this is discouraged and will be discussed in more detail in Chapter 5, *Delight Casual Users*, on page 71.

You can use the square-bracket syntax for a command's arguments as well. You should use [file_name] to indicate one file can be specified but that it isn't required, or you can use [file_name...] to indicate zero or more files would be accepted.

Documenting Options

Like the summary description of an app, one brief summary sentence should be sufficient to document each of its flags and switches. Each sentence should be as clear and to the point as possible. Again, sixty characters is a good limit to set, though it might be harder to hit for more complex options.

An argument to a flag should have a short, one-word description (or, if using multiple words, each separated with an underscore). If a flag has a default value, provide that value in the help string as well (we saw this in the documentation of the global flag -f that todo uses to locate the task list file). As with arguments for your app, if the argument to your flag is optional, surround its name with square brackets.

OptionParser and GLI more or less handle the formatting part for you, so you mainly need to focus on keeping your descriptions brief and to the point.

Documenting Commands in a Command Suite

Commands for a command suite require two bits of documentation: a one-line summary for the first level of help (e.g., the help shown by a command such as your_app help) and a longer description for the second level of help (e.g., from your_app help command_name).

As you might be able to guess by now, the one-line summary should be a very short description of what that command does; you can elaborate in the longer description. The GLI desc and long_desc methods provide a place for this documentation.

Command-specific arguments should follow the same conventions as those we discussed for the app's usage statement. The arg_name method in GLI provides a place to do this per-command.

Documenting Everything Else

An app's man page (or other extra documentation) provides more detail about how the app works and how its various options and arguments affect its behavior. This document should be sorted into sections, which will help to keep it organized and navigable (experienced UNIX users will look for certain section names so they can quickly scan the documentation). Table 2, *Common sections for your gem-man pages*, on page 51 outlines the common sections you might need and what goes in them (though you aren't limited to these sections; use your best judgment). Note that they are also listed *in the order that they should appear* in the man page and that you should include, at the very least, a "SYNOPSIS," "DESCRIPTION," and "EXAMPLE."

You should reuse documentation from your command-line interface here; typically your one-line summaries will be the first sentence of the paragraph that documents something. This saves you time, and it also helps connect the built-in help text to the more detailed documentation. Unfortunately, neither OptionParser nor GLI provide a way to autogenerate a man page so that your documentation can automatically be kept consistent. Perhaps you'll be inspired and create such a system.

3.5 Moving On

You should now know everything you need to know to make a command-line application that's helpful to newcomers as well as experts. All this is good news for your users; they'll have an easy time using your apps, but it's also good news for you as the developer; you can spend more time on your apps' actual functionality and less on formatting help text and documentation.

Users aren't the only entities who interact with your application, however. The system itself will be actually executing your application, and future developers may need to integrate your command-line apps into larger systems of automation (similar to how our database backup script integrates mysqldump). In the next chapter, we'll talk about how to make your apps interoperate with the system and with other applications.

Section	Meaning
SYNOPSIS	A brief synopsis of how to invoke your app on the command line. This should be similar to what the default banner is in OptionParser or what is output by GLI after the "Usage:" bit.
DESCRIPTION	A longer description of what your app does, why the user might use it, and any additional details. This section should be targeted at new users and written to help them understand how to use your app.
OPTIONS	A bullet list documenting each option. This is a chance to explain in more detail how the options work and what effect they have on your app's behavior.
EXAMPLES	One or more examples of using the app, including brief text explaining each example.
FILES	A list of files on the filesystem that the app uses (for example, todo would document the default to-do list file's location here).
ENVIRONMENT	A bullet list of any environment variables that affect the app's behavior.
BUGS	Known bugs or odd behaviors.
LICENSE	The name of the license and a reference to the full license text (you do not need to reproduce the entire license here).
AUTHOR	The authors of your app and their email addresses.
COPYRIGHT	The copyright information for your app.
SEE ALSO	Links to other commands or places on the Web that are relevant for your app.

Table 2—Common sections for your gem-man pages

## CHAPTER 4

Play Well with Others

In the previous two chapters, we learned how to write command-line applications that are easy to use and self-documenting. Such apps get their input via sophisticated and easy-to-create command-line interfaces and provide help text and documentation that let users get up to speed quickly. But the user at a terminal is only part of the story. Our app will be used by other apps, possibly even integrated into a sophisticated system. db_backup.rb is an example. We will probably want to run our database app nightly and we won't want to log into our server at midnight to do it, so we'll arrange for another app (such as cron) to run it for us. The fact is, we don't know who will run our app or how it will be run. What can we do to make sure it plays well with others?

On the command line, an app that "plays well with others" is an app that can be used easily by other apps directly or indirectly, alongside other apps, on the command line. db_backup.rb is a great example: it uses mysqldump and gzip to back up and compress a database. As we'll see, because both of these commands were designed to play well with others, it will be easy to make db_backup.rb a robust, easy-to-use app.

Much like making your app helpful and easy to use, making it play well with others is quite straightforward once you understand how command-line apps interact. Command-line apps communicate with each other over a small number of simple interfaces, three of which we'll go over in this chapter. The first is a simple messaging system between an app and an external command it invokes called *exit codes*; this messaging system allows us to send valuable information back to the app that called our app. The second is the output streams of an app; two standard output streams are available to all apps, and by following some simple conventions, apps can play well with each other in a simple and straightforward manner. We'll also talk about what sorts of output our app should be generating to make it work well in any situation. Along the way, we'll see how Ruby helps us take advantage of these features, all with built-in methods (like exit) and standard libraries (like Open3). Finally, we'll discuss a simple signaling mechanism that can be used to communicate with long-running or "daemon-style" apps.

First let's learn about exit codes, which are one of the simplest ways that programs interact with the system.

4.1 Using Exit Codes to Report Success or Failure

Every time a process finishes, it has the opportunity to return a single number to the process that called it. This is referred to as its *exit code* or *exit status*. A status of zero indicates that the program succeeded in what it was asked to do. Any other value indicates there was some sort of problem and that the command failed in some way. The shell variable $? allows us to examine the exit code of any app we run. We can use this to verify that mysqldump, the command our database backup app uses to perform the actual backup, exits zero on success and nonzero otherwise, like so:

```
$ mysqldump non_existent_database
No such database 'non_existent_database'
$ echo $?
1
$ mysqldump existing_database > existing_database.sql
$ echo $?
0
```

The first time it was called, mysqldump failed to perform a backup and exited with a 1. In the second invocation, it successfully backed up a database, so mysqldump exited with 0. We'd like to take advantage of this. As you'll recall, db_backup.rb uses Ruby's built-in system method to run mysqldump as follows:

```
play_well/db_backup/bin/db_backup.rb
auth = ""
auth += "-u#{options[:user]} " if options[:user]
auth += "-p#{options[:password]} " if options[:password]

database_name = ARGV[0]
output_file = "#{database_name}.sql"

command = "mysqldump #{auth}#{database_name} > #{output_file}"

system(command)
```

This code is pretty straightforward; we build up a few helper variables using our parsed command-line options, assemble them into a command string, and use system to execute the command. What happens if we use a database name that doesn't exist, as we did in our earlier example?

As we saw earlier, if we ask it to back up a nonexistent database, then mysqldump will fail and exit nonzero. Since the primary purpose of db_backup.rb is to back up a database, a failure to do so should result in a message to the user and a nonzero exit code. To make that happen, we need to check the exit code of mysqldump.

Accessing Exit Codes of Other Commands

Like bash, system sets the value of $? after a command is executed. Unlike bash, this value is not the exit code itself but an instance of Process::Status, a class that contains, among other things, the exit code. $? is intuitive if you've done a lot of bash programming, but it's otherwise a pretty bad variable name. To make our code a bit more readable, we can use a built-in library called English that will allow us to access this variable via the more memorable $CHILD_STATUS. We require the English built-in library first and can then use $CHILD_STATUS to examine the results of our system call.

play_well/db_backup/bin/db_backup.rb
```
require 'English'

puts "Running '#{command}'"
system(command)
➤ unless $CHILD_STATUS.exitstatus == 0
    puts "There was a problem running '#{command}'"
  end
```

By using the exit code, we can now get better information about the commands we run, which in turn allows us to give better information to the user. The error message we output isn't enough; our app needs to follow the exit code convention just like mysqldump does and exit with nonzero when it can't do what the user asked. Our current implementation always exits with zero, since that's the default behavior of any Ruby program that doesn't explicitly set its exit code. This means that no other app has any visibility to the success or failure of our backup.

Sending Exit Codes to Calling Processes

Setting the exit code is very simple. Ruby provides a built-in method, exit, that takes an integer representing the exit status of our app. In our case, if the mysqldump command failed, we need to fail, so we simply add a call to exit right after we print an error message.

play_well/db_backup/bin/db_backup.rb
```
puts "Running '#{command}'"
system(command)
➤ unless $CHILD_STATUS.exitstatus == 0
    puts "There was a problem running '#{command}'"
➤   exit 1
  end
```

Now if mysqldump experiences a problem, that problem bubbles up to whoever called db_backup.rb. Is there anywhere else in the code that would be considered an error? In Chapter 3, *Be Helpful*, on page 33, we added some code to check for a missing database name on the command line. When that happened, we displayed the help text as well as an error message. Although our app is being helpful by displaying both, it ultimately didn't do what it was asked and thus should exit nonzero. Let's add a call to exit to correct that omission:

play_well/db_backup/bin/db_backup.rb
```
option_parser.parse!
if ARGV.empty?
    puts "error: you must supply a database name"
    puts
    puts option_parser.help
➤   exit 2
  end
```

You'll notice that we used an exit code of 2 here, whereas we used 1 when mysqldump failed. Both of these values are nonzero and thus signal that our app failed, so what advantage do we get by using different values?

By associating a unique exit code with each known error condition, we give developers who use our app more information about failures, in turn giving them more flexibility in how they integrate our app into their system. For example, if another developer wanted to treat a failure to back up as a warning but a missing database name as an error, the following code could be used to implement this using db_backup.rb's exit codes:

```
system("db_backup.rb #{database_name}")
➤ if $?.exitstatus == 1
    puts "warn: couldn't back up #{database_name}"
  elsif $?.exitstatus != 0
    puts "error: problem invoking db_backup"
    exit 1
  end
```

Are There Any Standard Exit Codes?

As we mentioned, any nonzero exit code is considered an error. We also saw that we can use different error codes to mean different failures in our app. If there are any standard error codes, you may be wondering whether users of our app expect certain failures to always be encoded as certain values. There is no common standard across all command-line apps; however, some operating systems do recommend standard codes.

FreeBSD[a] has a list of recommendations in the man page for sysexits, available at http://www.freebsd.org/cgi/man.cgi?query=sysexits&sektion=3 (or by running man 3 sysexits on any FreeBSD system). For example, it recommends using the value 64 for a problem parsing the command line and using 77 for a lack of permission to access a resource.

The GNU Project[b] provides some less-specific recommendations, available at http://www.gnu.org/software/libc/manual/html_node/Exit-Status.html. Among their recommendations are to reserve numbers greater than 128 for special purposes and not to use the number of failures as the exit code.

Whether you choose to follow these conventions is up to you; however, it can't hurt to follow them if you have no reason not to, especially if your app is specific to FreeBSD or relies heavily on GNU apps to work. In the end, what's most important is that you clearly document the exit codes, regardless of which you use.

---

a. http://www.freebsd.org/
b. http://www.gnu.org/

Making the most of exit codes allows users of our app to use it in ways we haven't imagined. This is part of the beauty and flexibility of the command line, and exit codes are a big part of making that happen. By having each error condition represented by a different exit code, invokers have maximum flexibility in integrating our app into their systems.

There is a small limitation in using exit codes this way; only one piece of information can be sent back. Suppose we could detect several errors and wanted to let the caller know exactly what errors did, and didn't, occur?

Reporting Multiple Errors in the Exit Status

Although an exit code is only a single number, we can encode several bits of information in that number by treating it as a bitmask. In this strategy, each possible error is represented by a bit in the number we send back. For example, suppose that an invalid command-line option is represented by the bit in the 1 position and that the omission of the database name is represented by the bit in the 2 position. We could let the user know if they forgot the database *and* if they gave us a bad username like so:

```
➤ exit_status = 0
  begin
    option_parser.parse!
    if ARGV.empty?
      puts "error: you must supply a database name"
      puts
      puts option_parser.help
➤     exit_status |= 0b0010
    end
  rescue OptionParser::InvalidArgument => ex
    puts ex.message
    puts option_parser
➤   exit_status |= 0b0001
  end
➤ exit exit_status unless exit_status == 0

  # Proceed with the rest of the program
```

If it's been a while since you've done any bit-shifting, the |= operator tells Ruby to set a particular set of bits in the given number. We're using Ruby's handle binary literal syntax, so it's easy to see which bits are getting set. As we'll see in a minute, the & operator can be used to check whether a particular bit is set.

Also note that we must use the begin..rescue..end construct to detect an invalid command-line argument because option_parser.parse! will raise an OptionParser::InvalidArgument exception in that case. The message of that exception contains a reasonable error message explaining the problem. An invoker of our app could check for it like so:

```
system("db_backup.rb medium_client")
if $?.exitstatus & 0b0001
  puts "error: bad command-line options"
end
if $?.exitstatus & 0b0002
  puts "error: forgot the database name"
end
```

Note that the exit code is only an 8-bit number, so only eight possible errors can be encoded. This is probably sufficient for most uses, but it's a constraint to be aware of. The exit code strategy you use depends on the situation and the types of errors you can detect before exiting. Whichever method you decide on, be sure to document it!

Exit codes are all about communicating a result to a calling program. Many command-line apps, however, produce more output than just a single value. Our database backup app produces an output file, as well as messages about what the app is doing. Our to-do list app produces output in the form of our to-do items (for example, when we execute todo list). As we'll see, the form of our output can also communicate information to callers, as well as give them flexibility in integrating our apps into other processes.

4.2 Using the Standard Output and Error Streams Appropriately

In addition to the ability to return a single value to the calling program, all programs have the ability to provide output. The puts method is the primary way of creating output that we've seen thus far. We've used it to send messages to the terminal. A command line's output mechanism is actually more sophisticated than this; it's possible to send output to either of two standard *output streams*.

By convention, the default stream is called the *standard output* and is intended to receive whatever normal output comes out of your program. This is where puts sends its argument and where, for example, mysqldump sends the SQL statements that make up the database backup.[1]

The second output stream is called the *standard error* stream and is intended for error messages. The reason there are two different streams is so that the calling program can easily differentiate normal output from error messages. Consider how we use mysqldump in db_backup.rb:

play_well/db_backup/bin/db_backup.rb
```
command = "mysqldump #{auth}#{database_name} > #{output_file}"
system(command)
unless $CHILD_STATUS.exitstatus == 0
  puts "There was a problem running '#{command}'"
  exit 1
end
```

Currently, when our app exits with a nonzero status, it outputs a generic error message. This message doesn't tell the user the nature of the problem, only that something went wrong. mysqldump actually produces a specific message on its standard error stream. We can see this by using the UNIX redirect operator (>) to send mysqldump's standard output to a file, leaving the standard error as the only output to our terminal:

```
$ mysqldump some_nonexistent_database > backup.sql
mysqldump: Got error: 1049: Unknown database 'some_nonexistent_database' \
when selecting the database
```

---

1. A "database backup" produced by mysqldump is a set of SQL statements that, when executed, re-create the backed-up database.

backup.sql contains the standard output that mysqldump generated, and we see the standard error in our terminal; it's the message about an unknown database. If we could access this message and pass it along to the user, the user would know the actual problem.

Using Open3 to Access the Standard Output and Error Streams Separately

The combination of system and $CHILD_STATUS that we've used so far provides access only to the exit status of the application. We can get access to the standard output by using the built-in backtick operator (`) or the %x[] construct, as in stdout = %x[ls -l]. Unfortunately, neither of these constructs provides access to the standard error stream. To get access to both the standard output and the standard error independently, we need to use a module from the standard library called Open3.

Open3 has several useful methods, but the most straightforward is capture3. It's so-named because it "captures" the standard output and error streams (each as a String), as well as the status of the process (as a Process::Status, the same type of variable as $CHILD_STATUS). We can use this method's results to augment our generic error message with the contents of the standard error stream like so:

```
play_well/db_backup/bin/db_backup_2.rb
require 'open3'

puts "Running '#{command}'"
➤ stdout_str, stderr_str, status = Open3.capture3(command)

unless status.exitstatus == 0
  puts "There was a problem running '#{command}'"
➤ puts stderr_str
  exit -1
end
```

The logic is exactly the same, except that we have much more information to give the user when something goes wrong. Since the standard error from mysqldump contains a useful error message, we're now in a position to pass it along to the user:

```
$ db_backup.rb -u dave.c -p P@ss5word some_nonexistent_database
There was a problem running 'mysqldump -udavec -pP@55word \
some_nonexistent_database > some_nonexistent_database.sql'
➤ mysqldump: Got error: 1049: Unknown database 'some_nonexistent_database' \
➤ when selecting the database
```

Our use of the standard error stream allows us to "handle" any error from mysqldump, such as bad login credentials, which also generates a useful error message:

```
$ db_backup.rb -u dave.c -p password some_nonexistent_database
There was a problem running 'mysqldump -udavec -ppassword \
some_nonexistent_database > some_nonexistent_database.sql'
➤ mysqldump: Got error: 1044: Access denied for user 'dave.c'@'localhost'\
➤ to database 'some_nonexistent_database' when selecting the database
```

It's always good practice to capture the output of the commands you run and either send it to your app's output or store it in a log file for later reference (we'll see later why you might not want to just send such output to your app's output directly). Note that the version of Open3 that is included in Ruby 1.8 is not sufficient for this purpose; it hides the exit code from us. See *Open3 and Ruby 1.8*, on page 62 for a workaround if you're stuck using Ruby 1.8.

Now that we can read these output streams from programs we execute, we need to start writing to them as well. We just added new code to output an error message, but we used puts, which sends output to the standard output stream. We need to send our error messages to the right place.

Use STDOUT and STDERR to Send Output to the Correct Stream

Under the covers, puts sends output to STDOUT, which is a constant provided by Ruby that allows access to the standard output stream. It's an instance of IO, and essentially the code puts "hello world" is equivalent to STDOUT.puts "hello world". Ruby sets another constant, STDERR, to allow output to the standard error stream (see *STDOUT and STDERR vs. $stdout and $stderr*, on page 64 for another way to access these streams). Changing our app to use STDERR to send error messages to the standard error stream is trivial:

```
play_well/db_backup/bin/db_backup_3.rb
stdout_str, stderr_str, status = Open3.capture3(command)

unless status.success?
➤   STDERR.puts "There was a problem running '#{command}'"
➤   STDERR.puts stderr_str.gsub(/^mysqldump: /,'')
    exit 1
end
```

You could also use the method warn (provided by Kernel) to output messages to the standard error stream. Messages sent with warn can be disabled by the user, using the -W0 flag to ruby (or putting that in the environment variable RUBYOPTS, which is read by Ruby before running any Ruby app). If you want to be sure the user sees the message, however, use STDERR.puts.

Open3 and Ruby 1.8

Open3 in Ruby 1.8 is far less useful than the version that ships with Ruby 1.9.2. Its main failing is that it doesn't provide access to the exit code of our process. $CHILD_STATUS *is* set; however, the exitstatus method always returns zero, even if the underlying process exited nonzero.

If you can't use Ruby 1.9.2 but still want the benefits of 1.9.2's much-improved Open3 class, there is a library called Open4[a] that works with Ruby 1.8 to do exactly what we need. We could use it like so:

```
$ gem install open4

require 'open4'

pid, stdin, stdout, stderr = Open4::popen4(command)
_, status = Process::waitpid2(pid)
unless status.exitstatus == 0
  puts "There was a problem running '#{command}'"
  puts stderr
end
```

Open4 has the advantage of working on versions of Ruby 1.8 and newer. If you don't need 1.8 compatibility, using the built-in Open3 is preferred, since it's included with Ruby. However, it's nice to know that a third-party gem can do most of what we want on 1.8.

---

a.   https://github.com/ahoward/open4

Users of our app can now use our standard error stream to get any error messages we might generate. In general, the standard error of apps we call should be sent to our standard error stream.

We now know how to read output from and write output to the appropriate error stream, and we've started to get a sense of what messages go where. Error messages go to the standard error stream, and "everything else" goes to the standard output stream. How do we know what's an "error message" and what's not? And for our "normal" output, what format should we use to be most interoperable with other applications?

Use the standard error stream for any message that isn't the proper, expected output of your application. We can take a cue from mysqldump here; mysqldump produces the database backup, as SQL, to its standard output. Everything else it produces goes to the standard error. It's also important to produce *something* to the standard error if your app is going to exit nonzero; this is the only way to tell the user what went wrong.

The standard output, however, is a bit more complicated. You'll notice that mysqldump produces a very specific format of output to the standard output (SQL). There's a reason for this. Its output is designed to be handed off, directly, as input to another app. Achieving this is not nearly as straightforward as producing a human-readable error message, as we'll see in the next section.

4.3 Formatting Output for Use As Input to Another Program

If you've used the UNIX command line for even five minutes, you've used ls. It shows you the names of files in a particular directory. Suppose you have a directory of images with numeric names. ls nicely formats it for you:

```
$ ls
10_image.jpg   2_image.jpg   5_image.jpg   8_image.jpg
11_image.jpg   3_image.jpg   6_image.jpg   9_image.jpg
1_image.jpg    4_image.jpg   7_image.jpg
```

Suppose we want to see these files in numeric order. ls has no ability to do this; it sorts lexicographically, even when we use the invocation ls -1, which produces one file per line, in "sorted" order:[2]

```
$ ls -1
10_image.jpg
11_image.jpg
1_image.jpg
2_image.jpg
3_image.jpg
4_image.jpg
5_image.jpg
6_image.jpg
7_image.jpg
8_image.jpg
9_image.jpg
```

The UNIX command sort, however, *can* sort lines of text numerically if we give it the -n switch. If we could connect the output of ls to the input of sort, we could see our files sorted numerically, just how we'd like. Fortunately, the command line provides a way to do this. We follow our invocation of ls -1 with the pipe symbol (|) and follow *that* with a call to sort -n. This tells sort to use, as input, the standard output that came from ls:

---

2. Strictly speaking, the -1 is not required; we'll talk more about that in Chapter 5, *Delight Casual Users*, on page 71.

> ## STDOUT and STDERR vs. $stdout and $stderr
>
> In addition to assigning the constants STDOUT and STDERR to the standard output and error streams, respectively, Ruby also assigns the global variables $stdout and $stderr to these two streams (in fact, puts uses $stdout internally).
>
> Deciding which one to use is a mostly a matter of taste, but it's worth noting that by using the variable forms, you can easily reassign the streams each represents. Although reassigning the value of a constant is possible in Ruby, it's more straightforward to reassign the value of a variable. For example, you might want to reassign your input and output during testing to capture what's going to the standard error or output streams.
>
> We'll use the constant forms in this book, because we want to think of the standard output and error streams as immutable. The caller of our app should decide whether these streams should be redirected elsewhere, and if we ever need to send output to one of the streams *or* another IO instance, we would abstract that out, rather than reassign $stdin.

```
$ ls -1 | sort -n
1_image.jpg
2_image.jpg
3_image.jpg
4_image.jpg
5_image.jpg
6_image.jpg
7_image.jpg
8_image.jpg
9_image.jpg
10_image.jpg
11_image.jpg
```

If the creator of ls had not provided an output format that is one file per line, this would've been very difficult to do, and we would've had to write a custom program to parse the default output format of ls. The ability to connect these two commands is what makes the command line so powerful. You'll find that all UNIX commands obey this convention of formatting their output in a way to be used as input to another program. This is often referred to as the "UNIX Way," summed up neatly at faqs.org:[3]

> Expect the output of every program to become the input to another, as yet unknown, program. Don't clutter output with extraneous information. Avoid stringently columnar or binary input formats.

---

3.   http://www.faqs.org/docs/artu/ch01s06.html

How can we design our output to work as input to a program we know nothing about? It's actually pretty simple, once you're aware of a few conventions. Most command-line apps operate on one or more "things" that we can generically think of as *records*. As we'll see, each record should be on its own line. We got a hint of how handy that is in our earlier sorting example, in which a record in ls is a file. By using the -1 option, we got one record (file) per line. Currently, the output format of our todo list app is a multiline "pretty-printed" format that looks like so:

```
$ todo list
 1 - Clean kitchen
     Created:   2011-06-03 13:45
 2 - Rake leaves
     Created:   2011-06-03 17:31
     Completed: 2011-06-03 18:34
 3 - Take out garbage
     Created:   2011-06-02 15:48
 4 - Clean bathroom
     Created:   2011-06-01 12:00
```

This formatting might be pleasing to a human eye, but it's a nightmare as input to another program. Suppose we wanted to use our good friend sort to sort the list. As we've seen, sort sorts lines of text, so a naive attempt to sort our to-do list will lead to disastrous results:

```
$ todo list | sort
     Completed: 2011-06-03 18:34
     Created:   2011-06-01 12:00
     Created:   2011-06-02 15:48
     Created:   2011-06-03 13:45
     Created:   2011-06-03 17:31
 1 - Clean kitchen
 2 - Rake leaves
 3 - Take out garbage
 4 - Clean bathroom
```

If we could format each record (in our case, a task) on one line by itself, we could then use UNIX tools like sort and cut to manipulate the output for todo to get a properly sorted list. But beyond interoperability with standard UNIX tools, we want our app to be able to work with as many apps as possible, in ways we haven't thought of. This means that users can get the most out of our app and won't need to wait for us to add special features. The easiest way to make that happen is to spend some time thinking about how to format each record.

Format Output One Record per Line, Delimiting Fields

We can easily format our records for output one line at a time like so:

```
$ todo list
 1 Clean kitchen Created 2011-06-03 13:45
 2 Rake leaves Created 2011-06-03 17:31 Completed 2011-06-03 18:34
 3 Take out garbage Created 2011-06-02 15:48
 4 Clean bathroom Created 2011-06-01 12:00
```

This approach certainly follows our "one record per line" rule, but it's not that useful. We can't reliably tell where the task name stops and the created date begins. This makes it hard to use a command like cut to extract, say, just the task name. cut expects a single character to separate each field of our record. In our case, there is no such character; an app that wanted to extract the different fields from our tasks would need to have a lot of smarts to make it work.

If we format our output by separating each field with an uncommon character, such as a comma, parsing each record becomes a lot simpler; we just need to document which field is which so a user can use a command like cut or awk to split up each line into fields. We can demonstrate the power of this format by using a few UNIX commands to get a list of our task names, sorted alphabetically.

```
$ todo list
1,Clean kitchen,2011-06-03 13:45,
2,Rake leaves,2011-06-03 17:31,2011-06-03 18:34
3,Take out garbage,2011-06-02 15:48,
4,Clean bathroom,2011-06-01 12:00,
$ todo list | cut -d',' -f2
Clean kitchen
Rake leaves
Take out garbage
Clean bathroom
$ todo list | cut -d',' -f2 | sort
Clean bathroom
Clean kitchen
Rake leaves
Take out garbage
```

The code to do that is fairly trivial:

play_well/todo/bin/todo
```
complete_flag = completed ? "C" : "U"
printf("%d,%s,%s,%s,%s\n",index,name,complete_flag,created,completed)
```

By formatting our output in a general and parseable way, it can serve as input to any other program, and our app is now a lot more useful to a lot more users. A user of our app can accomplish her goals by sending our app's output to another app's input. Users get to use our app in new ways, and we don't have to add any new features!

There's one last problem, however. Suppose we wanted to use grep to filter out the tasks that have been completed. In our current format, a task is completed if it has a date in the fourth field. Identifying lines like this is a bit tricky, especially for simple tools like grep. If we add additional information in our output, however, we can make the job easier.

Add Additional Fields to Make Searching Easier

Even though users can see that a task is incomplete because the "completed date" field is omitted from its record, we can make life easier for them by making that information more explicit. To do that in our to-do app, we'll add a new field to represent the status of a task, where the string "DONE" means the task has been completed and "INCOMPLETE" means it has not.

```
$ todo list
1,Clean kitchen,INCOMPLETE,2011-06-03 13:45,
2,Rake leaves,DONE,2011-06-03 17:31,2011-06-03 18:34
3,Take out garbage,INCOMPLETE,2011-06-02 15:48,
4,Clean bathroom,INCOMPLETE,2011-06-01 12:00,
$ todo list | grep ",INCOMPLETE,"
1,Clean kitchen,INCOMPLETE,2011-06-03 13:45,
3,Take out garbage,INCOMPLETE,2011-06-02 15:48,
4,Clean bathroom,INCOMPLETE,2011-06-01 12:00,
```

Note that we include the field delimiters in our string argument to grep so we can be sure what we are matching on; we don't want to identify a field as incomplete because the word "INCOMPLETE" appears in the task name.

At this point, any user of our app can easily connect our output to another app and do things with our to-do list app we haven't thought of. Our app is definitely playing well with others. The only problem is that machine-readable formats tend not to be very human readable. This wasn't a problem with ls, whose records (files) have only one field (the name of the file). For complex apps like todo, where there are several fields per record, the output is a bit difficult to read.

A seasoned UNIX user would simply pipe our output into awk and format the list to their tastes. We can certainly leave it at that, but there's a usability concern here. Our app is designed to be used by a user sitting at a terminal. We want to maintain the machine-readable format designed for interoperability with other apps but also want our app to interoperate with its users.

Provide a Pretty-Printing Option

The easiest way to provide both a machine-readable output format and a human-readable option is to create a command-line flag or switch to specify the format. We've seen how to do this before, but here's the code we'd use in todo to provide this:

```
play_well/todo/bin/todo
desc 'List tasks'
command :list do |c|

  c.desc 'Format of the output'
  c.arg_name 'csv|pretty'
  c.default_value 'pretty'
  c.flag :format

  c.action do |global_options,options,args|
      if options[:format] == 'pretty'
        # Use the pretty-print format
      elsif options[:format] == 'csv'
        # Use the machine-readable CSV format
      end
  end
end
```

We've chosen to make the pretty-printed version the default since, as we've mentioned, our app is designed primarily for a human user. That might not be the case for every app, so use your best judgment as to what is appropriate.

Command-line options, exit codes, and output streams are great for apps that start up, do something, and exit. For long-running (or *daemon*) apps, we often need to communicate with the app without restarting it. This is done via an operating system feature called *signals*, which we'll learn about next.

4.4 Trapping Signals Sent from Other Apps

Our two example apps, db_backup.rb and todo, are not long-running apps. They start up very quickly and exit when they're done. While this is very common for command-line apps, there are occasions where we will need to write a long-running process. You may have a process that runs all the time, polling a message queue for work to do, or you may need to run a process that monitors other processes. Or, you might have a task that just takes a long time. In each case, you'll want a way for a user to send information to your running app.

The most common example is to stop an app from running. We do this all the time by hitting CTRL-C when an app is running in our terminal. This actually sends the app a *signal*, which is a rudimentary form of interprocess communication. By default, Ruby programs will exit immediately when they receive the signal sent by CTRL-C. This may not be what you want, or you may want to cleanly shut down things before actually exiting. To allow for this, Ruby programs can *trap* these signals.

To trap a signal, the module Signal, which is built in to Ruby, provides the method trap. trap takes two arguments: the signal to trap and a block of code to run when that signal is received by the program.

The POSIX standard (which is followed by both UNIX and Windows) provides a list of signals that can be trapped. There are many different signals—see a complete list at http://en.wikipedia.org/wiki/Signal_(computing)—but the signal we're generally interested in is SIGINT, which is sent by CTRL-C as well as by the kill command. For a long-running process, you should also trap SIGABRT and SIGQUIT, since those two signals, along with SIGINT, could be used to attempt to shut down your app.

Suppose we wanted to enhance db_backup.rb to clean up the database dump whenever the user kills it. This scenario could happen, because a database dump takes a long time. The current implementation of db_backup.rb will, if killed, exit immediately, leaving a partial dump file in the current directory. Let's fix that by trapping SIGINT, removing the database output file, and *then* exiting.

play_well/db_backup/bin/db_backup_3.rb
```
Signal.trap("SIGINT") do
  FileUtils.rm output_file
  exit 1
end
```

Cleaning up isn't the only thing you can do by trapping signals. You can use the signal system to create a control interface to modify a running app's behavior. For example, many daemon processes trap SIGHUP and reread their configuration. This allows such apps to reconfigure themselves without shutting down and restarting.

4.5 Moving On

So far, we've learned the nuts and bolts of creating an easy-to-use, helpful, and flexible command-line application. In this chapter, we've seen how exit codes can communicate success or failure to apps that call them. We've seen the importance of sending error messages to the standard error stream, and we've seen the amazing power of formatting our standard output as if it were destined to be input to another program. We've also seen how long-running apps can receive signals from users or other apps. These lessons are truly what makes the command line so infinitely extensible.

If all you did was follow these rules and conventions, you'd be producing great command-line apps. But, we want to make *awesome* command-line apps, and these rules and conventions can take us only so far. There are still a lot of open questions about implementing your command-line app. Our discussion of "pretty-printed" vs. "machine readable" formats is just one example: how should you decide which default to use? What about files that our app creates or uses; where should they live? Should we always use a one-letter name for our command-line options? When should we use the long-form names? How do we choose the default values for flags?

The answers to these questions aren't as clear-cut, but in the next chapter, we'll try to answer them so that your apps will provide the best user experience possible.

## CHAPTER 5

Delight Casual Users

So far, we've learned how to write easy-to-use, helpful command-line apps that interoperate well with other apps and systems. But in the previous chapter, we saw how subjective design decisions can be when we had to decide which output format of our to-do app would be the default. Choosing default values and behavior—as well as naming our commands, options, and arguments—is not as straightforward as using exit codes or sending output to the right place. These choices are design decisions that can profoundly affect how a user interacts with your app. Each decision nudges the user in one direction or the other, making some tasks simpler for the user to execute and some more difficult. In short, the right design decision can be the difference between a mediocre app and an awesome one.

It can be very difficult to know how to make these decisions and to understand the impact they will have on an app's behavior. Command-line applications, however, operate in a more constrained environment; the user interacts with our apps in limited ways, and the output that can be produced is similarly limited. This allows us to articulate some simple guiding principles and rules of thumb to help make these design decisions. In this chapter, we'll start to understand these principles and rules, all in the name of creating command-line applications that have an awesome user experience.

To help guide us in making design decisions, such as the names of options, the default values of arguments, or the default behavior of our app, we need a small set of principles we can refer to. Here are three guiding principles for designing command-line applications that we'll explore in this chapter:

- Make common tasks easy to accomplish.

- Make uncommon tasks *possible* (but not easy).

- Make default behavior nondestructive.

From these principles, we'll find there are many rules of thumb that we can apply to our designs. To discover what these are and see how to apply them, we'll examine the three main design elements of a command-line application: the names of the command-line options, the default values for flags and arguments, and the default behavior of the app itself.

We'll do this by refining our two running examples: db_backup.rb, the MySQL backup app, and todo, our simple to-do list manager. Let's get started with the first design decisions we'll face: the names of our options and commands.

5.1 Choosing Names for Options and Commands

In Chapter 2, *Be Easy to Use*, on page 13, we learned that OptionParser allows us to create multiple options that mean the same thing. We used this feature in our database backup script, db_backup.rb, by allowing both -i and --iteration to signify an "end-of-iteration" backup. Why does OptionParser have this feature, and why did we use it?

Naming Options

This question is better posed in two parts: "Why did we provide a short-form option?" and "Why did we provide a long-form option?" Short-form options allow frequent users who use the app on the command line to quickly specify things without a lot of typing. Long-form options allow maintainers of systems that use our app to easily understand what the options do without having to go to the documentation. Let's look at an example.

Suppose we've set up db_backup.rb to run nightly at 2 a.m. We've also set up our "end-of-iteration" backup to run on the first of the month at 2:30 a.m. We accomplish this by using cron, which is a common UNIX utility for running regularly scheduled commands. Suppose that Bob, a sysadmin who maintains the servers where we run our backups, wants to configure the system to perform automated maintenance on the first of the month. The first thing he'll do is look at cron's configuration to see what else is going on at the first of the month. He'll need to get a complete picture of what's been configured so he can decide how to get his job done. He'll see something like this:

```
00 02 * * 1-5  db_backup.rb -u dave.c -p P455w0rd small_client
30 02 1 * *    db_backup.rb -i -u dave.c -p P455w0rd small_client
```

(If you aren't familiar with cron, the format for the earlier crontab is as follows: the first five values tell cron when to run the command. The numbers represent, in order, minute, hour, day of month, month, and day of week. An asterisk is the symbol for "all," so the first line tells db_backup.rb to run every weekday

(1-5 as the fifth value) at 2 a.m. (the 00 and 02 as the first and second values, respectively). The second line tells cron to run our "end-of-iteration" backup at 2:30 a.m. on the first of the month.

Bob has never run db_backup.rb, and while he does understand that our dev team runs two types of backups (daily and "end of iteration"), the -i isn't going to mean anything to him. He'll have to find the documentation for db_backup.rb or go to the command line and run db_backup.rb --help. While we could have added a comment to the crontab entry, it's actually much clearer to use the long-form option:

```
00 02 * * 1-5  db_backup.rb -u dave.c -p P455w0rd small_client
➤ 30 02 1 * *   db_backup.rb --iteration -u dave.c -p P455w0rd small_client
```

Now Bob knows exactly what the second line is doing and why it's there. We could be even more conscientious and turn the long-form option into --end-of-iteration. Of course, we wouldn't change -i to -e; *i* is a good mnemonic for "iteration," which makes it a good name for the short-form version of the option.

This example illustrates the importance of good naming as well as the form of those names. This leads us to the following rules of thumb regarding naming your options:

- For short-form options, use a mnemonic that frequent users will easily remember. Mnemonics are a well-known learning technique that is common in command-line application user interfaces.

- Always provide a long-form option and use it in configuration or other scripts. This allows us to create very specific and readable command-line invocations inside configuration files or other apps. We saw how it helped Bob understand what was going on in cron's configuration; we want everyone to have this experience maintaining systems that use our apps.

- Name long-form options explicitly and completely; they are designed to be *read* more so than written. Users aren't going to frequently type out the long-form options, so it's best to err on the side of clarity.

Let's follow these guidelines and enhance db_backup.rb by renaming --iteration and adding long-form options for -u and -p:

make_easy_possible/db_backup/bin/db_backup.rb
```
opts.on("-i",
➤       "--end-of-iteration",
        'Indicate that this backup is an "iteration" backup') do
  options[:iteration] = true
end
```

```
opts.on("-u USER",
        "--username",
        "Database username, in first.last format") do |user|
  options[:user] = user
end

opts.on("-p PASSWORD",
        "--password",
        "Database password") do |password|
  options[:password] = password
end
```

Now our crontab is easy to read by just about anyone who sees it:

```
00 02 * * 1-5  db_backup.rb --username=dave.c \
                            --password=P455w0rd small_client
30 02 1 * *    db_backup.rb --end-of-iteration \
                            --username=dave.c \
                            --password=P455w0rd small_client
```

While we should always provide a long-form option, the converse isn't true; some options should have long-form names only and *not* short-form versions. The reason for this is to support our second guiding principle: while we want uncommon tasks or features to be possible, we don't want to make them easy.

The reason for this is twofold. First, there's the practical limitation of having only twenty-six letters and ten digits available for short-form option names (or fifty-two if you include uppercase, although using short-form options as mnemonics makes it hard to have both an -a and an -A that the user will remember). Any new short-form option "uses up" one of these characters. Since we want our short-form options to be mnemonics, we have to ask ourselves, "Is this new option worthy of using one of those letters?"

Second, there is a usability concern with using short-form options. The existence of a short-form option signals to the user that that option is common and encouraged. The absence of a short-form option signals the opposite—that using it is unusual and possibly dangerous. You might think that unusual or dangerous options should simply be omitted, but we want our application to be as flexible as is reasonable. We want to guide our users to do things safely and correctly, but we also want to respect that they know what they're doing if they want to do something unusual or dangerous.

Let's put this to use. db_backup.rb compresses the database backup file, but suppose a user didn't want to perform the compression? Currently, they have no way to do that. We're happy to add this feature, but it's not something we want to encourage; database backup files are quite large and can quickly fill the disk. So we allow this feature to be enabled with a long-form option only.

Let's add a new switch, using only a long-form name, and see how the app's help output affects the user experience:

```
make_easy_possible/db_backup/bin/db_backup.rb
options = {
  :gzip => true
}
option_parser = OptionParser.new do |opts|
  # ...
  opts.on("--no-gzip","Do not compress the backup file") do
    options[:gzip] = false
  end
end

$ ./db_backup.rb --help
Backup one or more MySQL databases

Usage: db_backup.rb [options] database_name

  -i, --end-of-iteration    Indicate that this backup is an "iteration" backup
  -u, --username USER       Database username, in first.last format
  -p, --password PASSWORD   Database password
      --no-gzip             Do not compress the backup file
```

Notice how the documentation for --no-gzip is set apart visually from the other options? This is a subtle clue to the user that this option is not to be frequently used. For apps with a lot of options, this visual distinction is a great way for users to quickly scan the output of --help to see which common options they might need: those with a short-form name.

Naming Commands in a Command Suite

For command suites, the names of commands should follow the same guidelines: all commands should have a clear, concise name. Common commands can have shorter mnemonics if that makes sense. For example, many command-line users are familiar with the ls command, and it is a mnemonic of sorts for "list." We can take advantage of this in our task-management app todo and provide ls as an alias for the list command. Since todo is a GLI-based app, we simply pass an Array of Symbol to command instead of just a Symbol:

```
make_easy_possible/todo/bin/todo
command [:list,:ls] do |c|

  # ...

end
```

Now frequent users can do todo ls:

```
$ todo help
usage: todo [global options] command [command options]

Version: 0.0.1

Global Options:
    -f, --filename=todo_file - Path to the todo file (default: ~/.todo.txt)
    --force-tty            -

Commands:
    done     - Complete a task
    help     - Shows list of commands or help for one command
➤   list, ls - List tasks
    new      - Create a new task in the task list
```

Naming can be difficult, but our guidelines around mnemonics, descriptive long-form options, and judicious use of short-form names can help. Now it's time to go one level deeper into a command-line app and talk about the default values for flags and arguments. An example of what we mean is the --filename global option to our to-do list management app, todo. Why did we choose ~/.todo.txt as a default; *should* we have chosen a default, and is that the best default value we could've chosen?

5.2 Choosing Default Values for Flags and Arguments

The existence of flags in an app's user interface serves our guiding principle of making uncommon things possible, and providing good defaults helps make common things easy. A sensible default communicates *your* intention of how to use your app, since the default value makes a particular usage of your app very simple (we'll see how to allow users to customize defaults in Chapter 6, *Make Configuration Easy*, on page 89). Let's see how to decide on good defaults both for the arguments given to flags and for the arguments to our app (see Chapter 2, *Be Easy to Use*, on page 13 if you need a quick review of the different parts of the command line).

Default Values for Flags

First, you should almost always have a default for flags; a flag that is required is not user-friendly and is burdensome for users to have to include on the command line every time they run your app. It's possible that your app is complex enough that it needs information from the user for which there is no good default. This is ideally rare, and we'll see some techniques to allow a user to set defaults in Chapter 6, *Make Configuration Easy*, on page 89, but, in general, consider a good default for every flag.

The default you choose is, obviously, dependent on what your app does and how the flag's value affects it. In other words, it is a design decision you'll have to make. An easy way to decide on a default value is to ask yourself "What default value would *I* prefer?" or "What default enables the most common behavior?"

You're presumably writing a command-line app for yourself or others like you, so this is as good a place to start as any. That being said, there are conventions for certain types of flags, such as a flag that takes a filename as an argument. Another common example is a flag that controls output formatting. Let's look at these two types of flags in more detail.

Flag Arguments That Represent Filenames

Many times, a flag's argument is a filename. An example of this is our to-do list app's global option --filename. We chose ~/.todo.txt as our default, meaning the file named .todo.txt, located in the user's home directory.

In general, files that represent data that persists across invocations of the app, such as a database or configuration file, should live in the user's home directory by default. This allows the app to be used by many users on a system without any chance of collisions (imagine if the default was the same file for all users; everyone's tasks would be mixed together!).

It's also common practice to use a leading period (.) in the filename so that the file is hidden by default in directory listings. This prevents the user from being distracted by your app's data and also reinforces that this file shouldn't be tampered with. There's less convention around the filename for databases, but for configuration files, it's customary to use the suffix .rc (see *The .rc Suffix*, on page 78 for the etymology of this suffix).

If a flag's argument is a filename but not a database or configuration file, you'll have to use your best judgment; however, keep in mind that many different users might use this app on the same system, so choose a default that is most appropriate or convenient for most users that won't cause collisions. For example, if your application produces a log file, then a location like /var/log/my_app.log would *not* be a good default; multiple users might contend for that common location. A better value would be ~/tmp/my_app.log. Another option would be to name the file using the current process identifier, available via $$ in any Ruby app: log_file = "/tmp/my_app_#{$$}.log". Note that if you are requireing English, as we did in Chapter 4, *Play Well with Others*, on page 53, you can use the more readable variable name $PROCESS_ID.

The .rc Suffix

Most UNIX commands use the suffix .rc for the name of configuration files. According to Wikipedia,[a] this extension isn't an acronym for "resource configuration" or "runtime configuration" but comes from a command called RUNCOM.

RUNCOM was created by Louis Pouzin for the Compatible Time-Sharing System (CTSS), which was one of the first time-sharing operating systems. RUNCOM was used to execute a series of commands in succession—a precursor to what we now call a *shell script*.

He is even credited with coining the term *shell*, as he describes in a post on the Internet from 2000[b] on the origins of the shell:

> After having written dozens of commands for CTSS, I reached the stage where I felt that commands should be usable as building blocks for writing more commands, just like subroutine libraries. Hence, I wrote "RUNCOM", a sort of shell driving the execution of command scripts, with argument substitution. The tool became instantly most popular [sic], as it became possible to go home in the evening while leaving behind long runcoms executing overnight.
>
> ...
>
> Without being invited on the subject, I wrote a paper explaining how the Multics command language could be designed with [the] objective [of using commands somehow like a programming language]. And I coined the word "shell" to name it.

Although RUNCOM (and CTSS) has long-been retired from regular use, its legacy lives on both as the name for user-specific configuration files and as the basis for the UNIX start-up scripts, typically located in /etc/rc.d.

---

a.   http://en.wikipedia.org/wiki/Rc_file
b.   http://www.multicians.org/shell.html

Flag Arguments That Control Output Formatting

We saw in Chapter 4, *Play Well with Others*, on page 53 that todo's list command takes the flag --format to control the output format. This is a pretty common type of flag and can be seen in several popular Ruby applications, such as Cucumber[1] and RSpec.[2] Choosing the default format can be tricky, especially when you have support for more than just a basic format and a pretty format.

In the case of todo, we chose "pretty" as the default, because this makes the simplest and most common case of using the app very easy: a user is using their terminal and wants to manage a to-do list. The pretty format is easy for human eyes, and we don't expect the app to be called from another system (like cron).

---

1.   http://cukes.info
2.   http://www.rspec.info

What if your app supports multiple formats, like Cucumber does? At the time of this writing, Cucumber supports eleven different output formats. The default is a colored, indented format that shows passing, pending, and failing tests in green, yellow, and red, respectively. Why is *that* the default?

This default represents a design decision by the creators of Cucumber to motivate a certain type of behavior and use of the app. Cucumber wants you to do test-driven development, where you write a (failing) test first and, knowing it will fail, run it. With the default output format, this produces some red text. You then write code to make the tests pass, gradually turning the red output into green output. Once all your output is green ("like a cuke"), your job is done.

Cucumber's choice of default output format is very powerful; it makes it very obvious what the tool is doing and how you "should" use it (this isn't to say that you should always use colorful output; in general, you shouldn't, but we'll see in Chapter 10, *Add Color, Formatting, and Interactivity*, on page 153 when to do so and how). This makes the common way of using the app simple. Cucumber makes the uncommon things possible, however, by including "machine-friendly" formats, such as JSON.[3] What you should do, when faced with choosing a default output format, is to think about what your app does and how *you* want users to use it. Choose the output format that closely matches that use case.

We've talked about default values for flags, but what about default values for our app's arguments?

Default Values for the App's Arguments

Although many command-line apps' arguments are a list of files, an app's arguments really represent some sort of input. In the common case of arguments-as-filenames, these names represent sources of input. In the case of our to-do list app, todo, the argument to the new command *is* the input (the name of a new task). In both of these cases, the best default value for this input is the content of the *standard input stream.*

Much like the standard output and standard error streams, the standard input stream is available to all applications and is used to access any input piped into the app. When we piped the output of ls into sort, sort read this information from its standard input stream. (If no input is piped into the command, the terminal will allow the user to enter text, which becomes the

---

3.   http://en.wikipedia.org/wiki/JSON

ARGF: Automatically Read from Files or Standard Input

Many command-line apps take their input from a list of files and use the standard input as the default if no files are provided on the command line. Almost every standard UNIX command works this way, and because it is so common, Ruby provides ARGF to make this easier.

Let's take a simple app to sort the lines of any files, or the standard input, much like the UNIX command sort:

make_easy_possible/sort.rb
```ruby
#!/usr/bin/env ruby
def read_file(io,lines)
  io.readlines.each { |line| lines << line.chomp }
end
lines = []
if ARGV.empty?
  read_file(STDIN,lines)
else
  ARGV.each { |file| read_file(File.open(file),lines) }
end
puts lines.sort.join("\n")
```

With ARGF, we can eliminate both the check for files on the command and the iteration over those files if they are included.

make_easy_possible/sort_argf.rb
```ruby
#!/usr/bin/env ruby

lines = []

ARGF.readlines.each { |line| lines << line.chomp }

puts lines.sort.join("\n")
```

ARGF includes all the logic to figure out where to get input from and will iterate over every file provided on the command line using the standard input if none was provided. ARGF even provides methods to know where you are in the list of files. filename returns the name of the file currently being processed, and lineno returns the line number within that file. This means you can provide good error messaging to the user when processing files in this manner.

To learn more about ARGF, consult its documentation page at http://www.ruby-doc.org/core-1.9.3/ARGF.html.

standard input to the app) In Ruby, the standard input is available via the constant STDIN.

For apps that use a list of files as their source of input, Ruby provides the class ARGF in its standard library, which implements the exact behavior described here. See *ARGF: Automatically Read from Files or Standard Input*, on page 80 for more on how to use this.

How could todo use the standard input stream as a default source of input? Consider setting up your to-do list for the first time. You probably have a lot of tasks to input initially, and given the way todo is implemented, you'd have to call todo new for each one of them. If, on the other hand, todo new accepted task names from the standard input, you could enter them much more quickly, like so:

```
$ todo new
Rake Leaves
Take out trash
Clean garage
Put away Dishes
^D
$ todo list
1 - Rake Leaves
    Created: Mon Aug 15 21:01:35 EDT 2011
2 - Take out trash
    Created: Mon Aug 15 21:01:35 EDT 2011
3 - Clean garage
    Created: Mon Aug 15 21:01:35 EDT 2011
4 - Put away Dishes
    Created: Mon Aug 15 21:01:35 EDT 2011
```

To implement this, we simply check whether the argument list given to the new command is empty and, if so, use the readlines method on STDIN to read each new task, one at a time. We'll let the user know that we're doing this so they don't get confused when the app patiently waits for input. In our continued desire to be helpful, we'll add a check to see whether the standard input contained tasks and send a message to the user if no tasks were created.

```
make_easy_possible/todo/bin/todo
    c.action do |global_options,options,task_names|
      File.open(global_options[:filename],'a+') do |todo_file|
➤       if task_names.empty?
➤         puts "Reading new tasks from stdin..."
➤         task_names = STDIN.readlines.map { |a| a.chomp }
➤       end
        tasks = 0
        task_names.each do |task|
          todo_file.puts [task,Time.now].join(',')
          tasks += 1
        end
➤       if tasks == 0
➤         raise "You must provide tasks on the command-line or standard input"
➤       end
      end
    end
```

The first block of highlighted lines checks whether task_names is empty and, if so, assigns it to each line of the standard input stream. Since these strings contain newlines, we use one of Ruby's famous one-liners to remove them by combining map, which maps array elements, with chomp, which removes newlines from the ends of strings.

The final highlighted bit of code shows our helpful error handling. Recall that in a GLI-based app, we can safely raise an exception; our app will exit nonzero, and the exception's message will be shown to the user (without the nasty backtrace).

If your app's arguments don't represent input or don't locate input for your app to process, a default value for its arguments might not make sense, though it's still worth considering. ls's arguments could be thought of as having a default of "the current directory." That default makes a lot of sense for ls because it's nondestructive and represents the normal, expected use case of ls: list the files in the current directory. There's no better example of making the common things easy. It might not be this straightforward for your app, but ideally we've given you some things to think about.

Now that we know how to name and set defaults for options, flags, and arguments, let's take our final step in understanding our guiding principles: default behavior.

5.3 Deciding Default Behavior

The default behavior is the behavior of our app in the absence of options; for example, db_backup.rb's default behavior is to compress database backups. Choosing the best default behavior is highly dependent on what your app does; however, there are two behaviors common to many command-line apps: modifying the system and producing output. Let's look at these two common behaviors to see how we apply our guiding principles to choosing default behavior.

We'll tackle modifying the system first, because it's the most common and the most important. By "modifying the system," we mean the creation, modification, and removal of files. This is where we finally apply our third guiding principle: "Don't be destructive by default."

Preventing Destructive Actions by Default

One of the most destructive commands on any UNIX system is rm; it deletes files. When you just type rm on the command line, however, nothing bad happens:

```
$ rm
usage: rm [-f | -i] [-dPRrvW] file ...
   unlink file
# => Hard drive NOT deleted
```

rm is not only helpful (as we've come to expect from great applications) but also nondestructive by default; nothing changed in our environment or on our machine from having run rm without any arguments. rm will even go so far as to ask permission before deleting a file that you own but that doesn't have write permissions. Our apps need to take the same care with their users' data as rm and prevent destructive behavior by default; however, we *do* want to allow such behavior in our continued effort to making uncommon or dangerous things possible.

Unless you're writing an app that deletes files, it might not be clear what's destructive and what isn't. A good rule of thumb is to think of destructive behavior as any irreversible action that occurs outside of the normal operations of the application. For example, adding a new task using todo new is not destructive; adding a task is the entire point of the new command. If db_backup.rb overwrote an existing backup without asking permission, however, *that* would be destructive.

Thinking about which behavior of an app is destructive is a great way to differentiate the common things from the uncommon things and thus drive some of your design decisions. Any feature that does something destructive shouldn't be a feature we make easy to use, but we *should* make it possible.

Let's change db_backup.rb to avoid, but allow, its currently destructive behavior. First, we'll check for an existing file before we start backing up and exit nonzero with an error message in that case. Second, we'll add a new flag, --force, that will allow skipping this check. This requires three distinct changes to our app.

make_easy_possible/db_backup/bin/db_backup.rb
```
option_parser = OptionParser.new do |opts|
  # ...
① opts.on("--[no-]force","Overwrite existing files") do |force|
    options[:force] = force
  end

end
auth = ""
auth += "-u#{options[:user]} " if options[:user]
auth += "-p#{options[:password]} " if options[:password]

database_name = ARGV[0]
output_file = "#{database_name}.sql"
```

```
command = "/usr/local/mysql/bin/mysqldump " +
            "#{auth}#{database_name} > #{output_file}"
```

```
② if File.exists? output_file
     if options[:force]
③      STDERR.puts "Overwriting #{output_file}"
     else
       STDERR.puts "error: #{output_file} exists, use --force to overwrite"
       exit 1
     end
   end
```

There's a lot going on here to make db_backup.rb nondestructive by default but without sacrificing the improvements we've made to make it an awesome app.

① Here, we add the --force option, but we also allow for --no-force to explicitly call out the default behavior on the command line. In a similar vein to accepting long-form options for readability in automation scripts, adding "negatable" switches can be advantageous. When someone sees --no-force as a switch to db_backup.rb in an automation script, they'll instantly know that the app is going to avoid being destructive without having to check the documentation about what the default behavior is.

② Here, we implement the basic logic to check for the file's existence and either exit with an error or allow the file to be overwritten, based on the value of options[:force].

③ Notice here how we still message the user (using the standard error stream, where such messages should go) that we're overwriting a file. It's always a good idea for an app to let the user know something destructive is happening, even when the user explicitly requested it.

Preventing destructive behavior is the most important default behavior your app can have. The second common behavior we want to look at is how it produces output. If your app produces output in a user-selectable format, choosing the default is important, and you should make that choice based on where that output is going.

Choosing the Best Default Output Format Based on Context

In Chapter 4, *Play Well with Others*, on page 53, we chose the "pretty" output format as the default. It turns out, we can be smarter about the format of our output by taking into account the way in which our app was invoked. ls does this; we saw previously that the -1 option tells ls to format its output one file per line, which we used to put ls into a pipeline. ls will use this format by default *if its output is sent to a file or another application*. This is an excellent example of how ls makes two common things simple through default behavior: when using ls at the terminal, we see a nicely formatted output format. When using it as part of a pipeline, it uses a more machine-friendly format.

We want our apps to do this, as well. In general, we don't want formatted or colorful output going to files or to the input of another application by default; we want to use the machine-friendly format in these cases. Let's enhance todo to choose its default format based on where its output is going.

To determine where the output is going, we can use the method tty? of the IO class to see whether the output is a terminal or not (TTY is an abbreviation for a teletypewriter[4] but is used in UNIX systems to refer to the terminal). Since STDOUT is an instance of IO, we can call tty? on it to find out where our output is going. Based on that, we can choose the default format.

```
make_easy_possible/todo/bin/todo
desc 'List tasks'
command [:list,:ls] do |c|

  c.desc 'Format of the output (pretty for TTY, csv otherwise)'
  c.arg_name 'csv|pretty'
➤ # explicit default removed
  c.flag :format

  c.action do |global_options,options,args|
➤   if options[:format].nil?
➤     if STDOUT.tty?
         options[:format] = 'pretty'
       else
         options[:format] = 'csv'
       end
     end

     # ...

  end
end
```

Note that we removed the explicit default value for the --format flag. This way, we can check whether it's nil (meaning the user didn't provide a value for it on the command line), and then check whether STDOUT is a terminal. Also note that since we removed the call to default_value, we had to augment the help text to explain how the default value is chosen.

---

4. http://en.wikipedia.org/wiki/Teletypewriter

Avoiding destructive behavior and sensibly choosing output formats are the most common types of behavior you'll need to consider for any given command-line app, but your app will do many other things. Choosing sensible defaults for them is dependent on the specifics of your app; these are design decisions you'll have to make. They will communicate to your users how your app should be used. As with the other issues we've discussed in this chapter, an easy way to choose appropriate default behavior is to think about how *you* want to use the app.

5.4 Moving On

Starting with our guiding principles of making common tasks easy, making uncommon tasks possible, and avoiding destructive behavior, we've discovered several guidelines to help us design our apps for an awesome user experience. They're summarized in the following list. Overall, you want to have an *opinion* about how your app is supposed to work and reflect that opinion in the names and defaults you choose and how your app behaves.

Use short-form option names only for common and nondestructive options.
Short-form options are easy to use and should affect only common behaviors; this reinforces the desired usage patterns of your app. Options available only in long form indicate to the user that they are uncommon or dangerous.

Short-form options should be mnemonics for the behavior they control.
Mnemonics are a common and easy way to help users remember things.

Always provide a long-form option, and use it when scripting your app.
Long-form options' verbose nature allows users reading invocations of your app to better understand what's being configured by the options.

Long-form options should be as clear as possible; don't skimp on letters.
Long-form options are designed to be well-understood by infrequent users, so they need to be descriptive.

For command suites, use abbreviations or mnemonics as aliases for common commands.
Frequent users will appreciate using two- or three-character aliases for common commands to your command suite, such as ls for list or cp for copy. These short-form aliases also help to reinforce what the common commands are.

Files that configure or drive the behavior of your app and persist across invocations should be located, by default, in the user's home directory, and they should be hidden (i.e., they should start with a .).

> The user's home directory is a safe sandbox that allows your app to create and manage files without fear of clashing with other users on the system. Hiding them is common practice so the user doesn't see them in directory listings.

Name files uniquely and in common locations (such as /tmp) to avoid collisions.

> Occasionally, you will need to create files in locations outside of the user's home directory. By using unique information, such as the process identifier, in filenames, you ensure that the app behaves well and doesn't interfere with other users of the app.

Use the standard input stream as the default source for input.

> Accepting input from the standard input stream allows your app to be more easily used in a pipeline and thus allows it to play well with others. It's also the default that most command-line apps use, so this will be expected by seasoned command-line users.

Do not delete or overwrite files as a side effect of what your app does without explicit instructions from the user (typically via a command-line switch).

> Respect users' data; they will trust and use your app more if it's well-behaved and doesn't cause irreversible damage to their environment.

Choose the output form of your app based upon the destination of the output.

> Even if your app produces human-friendly output by default, when that output is redirected to a file or to the input of another app, default to a machine-readable format. Using the context of where the output is going optimizes your app, making two common cases very simple.

What if users don't like our defaults? For example, what if a db_backup.rb user wants the backup file to be overwritten all the time and isn't happy about typing --force on the command line all the time? What if a todo user doesn't like new tasks being added with the lowest priority? Is there a way to make the experience of these users just as good as for everyone else?

In the next chapter, we'll learn how to make our applications configurable in an easy way that will allow users to customize the default behavior of our apps, all without sacrificing ease of use, helpfulness, or interoperability.

## CHAPTER 6

Make Configuration Easy

In the previous chapter, we learned how the design decisions we make provide direction to our users about how to use our apps. But, what about advanced users, who use our apps regularly but in unusual ways? Can we accommodate their requirements without sacrificing the usability we've worked so hard to build into our apps?

The answer is yes, and this chapter is about making that happen via external configuration, which is to say configuration that isn't part of the app but that the app can access at runtime (often referred to as *rc files* by old-school UNIX hackers; see *The .rc Suffix*, on page 78 for the history of that name).

We'll see how you can use a simplified text format called YAML to store and manage this configuration and how easy it is to access in your app via the Ruby standard library. We'll then see how this applies to a command-suite application, finishing up with a discussion about how the use of configuration files affects your application design, along with some approaches you can take to keep your app easy to use and maintain.

6.1 Why External Configuration?

In Chapter 5, *Delight Casual Users*, on page 71, we talked about making uncommon or dangerous things difficult to use *on purpose*. It might seem that the simplest solution to allowing power users to have easy access to these features is to make them easy to use. This is not the case and will result in a more complex "kitchen-sink" application that tries to do everything.

Our apps have a purpose, and the way we design them is our opinion on how they can best realize that purpose. This "opinion" is what allows new users to understand and use our app and what makes our app easy to use for the majority of users. We want to maintain this ease of use for everyday users while not complicating the work of power users.

The way to do this is to externalize aspects of our application's behavior into a configuration file. This way, power users can adjust things how they would like. External configuration gives us the best of both worlds; typical users get the ease of use we've designed in, and power users, with a bit of up-front work, get to use the app just as simply but get their desired behavior.

6.2 Reading External Configuration from Files

External configuration allows a user to control the behavior of an app without using command-line options and arguments, in a more transparent and persistent way. The intent is to give users the ease of use provided by the default behavior but customized for their needs.

As an example, suppose Bob, our sysadmin, is using db_backup.rb to test the effect of changing the settings of a MySQL server. Bob wants to see how these settings affect the speed with which db_backup.rb can complete a backup. Bob is not particularly interested in the backup file that results, only the speed with which it's produced. To do this, Bob will need to run db_backup.rb like so:

```
$ db_backup.rb --username=bob.sysadmin --password=P@ss!w0rd --force big_client
```

For Bob to type --force, along with his username and password every time he runs the application, is tedious. We want Bob to be able to create a configuration file and get the same behavior with just this invocation:

```
$ db_backup.rb big_client
```

Currently, the default values for --username and --password are nil, and the default for --force is false. We want to allow Bob to override these defaults via an external file that our app will read at start-up. The canonical format for that in Ruby apps is YAML.

Using YAML as a Configuration File Format

YAML (which is a recursive acronym for YAML Ain't Markup Language) is a text-based format that's useful for storing structured data. Ruby includes a built-in module (naturally called YAML) that makes it very easy to translate YAML into Ruby objects and back again. As an example, here's what db_backup.rb's default options look like in our code:

Why Not XML?

XML is a more widely used format than YAML for configuring things. Almost every piece of open source Java software is configured with XML. Although YAML is quite prolific in the Ruby community, there's another reason we're recommending it here: human-friendliness. Here's Bob's config file in XML:

```
<configuration>
    <gzip>false</gzip>
    <force>false</force>
    <user>Bob</user>
    <password>Secr3t!</password>
</configuration>
```

As you can see, there's more syntax/markup than there is data. The YAML version has less than half the amount of "noise" compared to the XML version. The result is a file that is very clear, easy to read, and easy to edit. This is the exact use case we want to enable with external configuration files.

We're not saying that YAML is better than XML in every situation, but it's far superior as a configuration file format, especially for simple applications like command-line apps.

make_config_easy/db_backup/bin/db_backup.rb

```
options = {
  :gzip => true,
  :force => false,
}
```

Here's how YAML would serialize them:

```
---
:gzip: true
:force: false
```

It looks *almost* like plain text; there's not much syntax there at all. The file starts with three dashes (which is simply a requirement of the format) and is then made up of key-value pairs. A key's name starts at the first column and ends at the first colon (obviously not counting the colon in the first column). When Ruby deserializes these keys, since they start with colons, it will turn them into Symbols instead of Strings. The values will get translated appropriately, as well. In this case, both values are booleans, but strings and numbers can be used and will be converted to the appropriate type. (YAML supports much richer encodings than just key-value pairs. The spec on http://yaml.org has a complete description, but, for our purposes, all we need to know are the basics.)

What we'd like to do is allow Bob to create a file like so:

```
---
:gzip: false
:force: true
:user: "Bob"
:password: "Secr3t!"
```

When he runs db_backup.rb, we'd like it to read this file and use it for its default option values, replacing the built-in ones.

Reading Defaults from a YAML-Based Configuration File

To allow Bob to override db_backup.rb's built-in defaults, we'll need to replace them *before* we parse the command line. To do that, we'll need to add a new step after the built-in defaults are set but before we start parsing. This step will read our configuration as a Hash and merge it with our defaults, overriding any defaults in our app with the user's external configuration. Before doing this, we need to figure out where this file comes from.

As we discussed in Chapter 5, *Delight Casual Users*, on page 71, configuration files should go in the user's home directory and be "hidden" (i.e., their names should be preceded by a period). We'll use the double-suffix .rc.yaml to indicate that this file is configuration (.rc) but that it's structured as YAML (.yaml).

Once we've checked that the file exists, we use the method YAML.load_file to deserialize the file into our default options Hash:

make_config_easy/db_backup/bin/db_backup.rb
```
require 'yaml'
options = {
  :gzip => true,
  :force => false,
}
CONFIG_FILE = File.join(ENV['HOME'],'.db_backup.rc.yaml')
if File.exists? CONFIG_FILE
  config_options = YAML.load_file(CONFIG_FILE)
  options.merge!(config_options)
end
option_parser = OptionParser.new do |opts|
  # ...
```

This is the only code we need to change; the defaults Bob configures override the built-in ones, but Bob can still override these on the command line.

As long as Bob places his configuration file in ~/.db_backup.rc.yaml, he no longer needs to specify anything on the command line. Although he's using db_backup.rb in an unusual way, it's still easy for him to get his work done.

YAML is very readable and editable, but it might be hard for the user to create this file correctly. The user might not know that the first line must have three dashes or that the options must be preceded by colons. Keeping with our goal of being helpful, we should create this file for the user if it doesn't exist.

Generating a YAML Configuration File for Users

By creating a configuration file for users automatically, we keep them from having to get the YAML syntax just right and understanding what options are available. What we want to do is create a standard configuration file that has all of the available options, each set to their default value, even if that default is nil.

Since we're already checking for the existence of the config file, we can add an else condition to create it. We'll also need to be explicit about options whose default value is nil. Although our code won't care if an option is omitted from the options Hash or mapped explicitly to nil, having each option mapped to a value will ensure each option shows up in the resulting YAML file.

`make_config_easy/db_backup/bin/db_backup.rb`
```ruby
options = {
  :gzip => true,
  :force => false,
➤ :'end-of-iteration' => false,
➤ :username => nil,
➤ :password => nil,
}

if File.exists? CONFIG_FILE
  options_config = YAML.load_file(CONFIG_FILE)
  options.merge!(options_config)
➤ else
➤ File.open(CONFIG_FILE,'w') { |file| YAML::dump(options,file) }
➤ STDERR.puts "Initialized configuration file in #{CONFIG_FILE}"
➤ end
```

Note that we let the user know we created this file, and we did so on the standard error stream, where such messages should go. Now, when the user runs db_backup.rb the first time, the following configuration file will be generated:

```
---
:gzip: true
:force: false
:"end-of-iteration": false
:username:
:password:
```

The user can easily see what configuration options are available and how to format them. It's also worth pointing out that the ability to control the app via configuration makes it doubly important that our switches are negatable (i.e., have the [no-] form). Thinking about Bob and his unusual use of db_back-up.rb, if he wanted to do a normal backup and there was no --no-force switch, he'd have to manually edit his config file.

We've seen how easy it is to generate this file, but should we? If your app has a lot of options (making it more likely to be configured externally), you should generate this file if it doesn't exist. Still, you may not want your app writing files that the user didn't request to be written. In this case, include a description and example of the format and options in the man page.

Configuring defaults for a command-line app is straightforward, and with just a few lines of code, we have everything we need. What about command suites?

6.3 Using Configuration Files with Command Suites

Suppose we've enhanced our todo app to sync our tasks with an external task management service like JIRA.[1] We created todo as a lightweight replacement for such systems, but we still might want to send tasks to and from this system to facilitate collaboration with others on our team. We'd need at least three new global options: a URL where JIRA is running, a username, and a password to access it. Suppose further that the new command will require the user to provide a group name to allow JIRA to properly file the ticket (a group might be something like "corporate web site" or "analytics database"). Let's assume we've added these features, as shown in this sample help output:

```
$ todo help
usage: todo [global options] command [command options]

Version: 0.0.1

Global Options:
    -f, --filename=todo_file - Path to the todo file (default: ~/.todo.txt)
    --url                    - URL to JIRA
    --username               - Username for JIRA
    --password               - Password for JIRA

Commands:
    done        - Complete a task
    help        - Shows list of commands or help for one command
```

---

1. http://www.atlassian.com/jira

```
    list         - List tasks
    new          - Create a new task in the task list
$ todo help new
new [command options] [task_name...]
    Create a new task in the task list

    Command Options:
      -f                     - put the new task first in the list
      -p priority            - set the priority of the new task, 1 being
                               the highest
      --group group_name - group for JIRA
```

While this is a great feature that we'll use frequently, it's made our app a bit cumbersome to use:

```
$ todo --url=http://jira.example.com --username=davec \
      --password=S3cr3tP@ss new --group "analytics database" \
      "Create tables for new analytics"
```

We might not even provide this feature because of the complexity of the command-line syntax. External configuration solves this usability problem. Just as we did with Bob, if we can make these options configured in a file that todo will read, we don't have to specify them every time. Our JIRA server location, name, password, and group are probably not going to change all that often, so these are perfect candidates for us to configure externally.

The flattened structure we've encoded in YAML thus far isn't going to work. Bob configured db_backup.rb with a simple list of key-value pairs. For a command suite, different commands can use options of the same name, or a global option might be the same name as a command-specific one (as is the case with -f; it's used as a global option as well as an option for new).

Fortunately, YAML can handle this situation easily. We've seen only the most basic YAML format; YAML can store almost *any* Ruby object, including a slightly deeper Hash. Suppose we think of our options as a hierarchy; at the top are all the global options. Each command creates its own level in the hierarchy containing options specific to that command. In YAML, we can store it like so:

```
---
:filename: ~/.todo.txt
:url: http://jira.example.com
:username: davec
:password: S3cr3tP@ss
commands:
  :new:
    :f: true
    :group: Analytics Database
```

```
:list:
  :format: pretty

:done: {}
```

YAML doesn't ignore the indentation but rather uses it to re-create Ruby objects. The indented key-value list underneath commands is treated as a Hash mapped to by the string "commands." It's still easy to read and write by the user but rich enough to hold all of our options in code. Deserializing this into Ruby gives us the following Hash:

```
{
  :filename  => '~/.todo.txt'
  :url       => 'http://jira.example.com'
  :username  => 'davec'
  :password  => 'S3cr3tP@ss'
  'commands' => {
    :new       => {
      :f           => true
      :group       => 'Analytics Database'
    }
    :list:     => {
      :format      => 'pretty'
    }
    :done      => {}
    }
  }
}
```

Using a Hash like this, we can easily tell which options are which. Applying the user's external configuration is the same as we've already seen with db_backup.rb. We could then use these values with GLI's default_value method to let the user change the defaults via external configuration, as such:

```
➤ defaults = YAML.load_file(file)

  desc "Path to the todo file"
  arg_name "todo_file"
➤ default_value defaults[:filename] || "~/.todo.txt"
  flag [:f,:filename]

  # ...
  command :new do |c|
    c.desc 'set the priority of the new task, 1 being the highest'
    c.arg_name 'priority'
➤   c.default_value defaults[:p]
    c.flag :p

    # ...
  end
```

GLI actually can do this for us, with just one line of code. Instead of choosing a file format, adding the code to parse the file, and then applying it to each global and command-specific option, GLI bakes this concept in.

If you call the config_file method, giving it the path to the config file, GLI will do two things. First, it will look for that file in the nested YAML format we described earlier and apply its contents as defaults for all options. Second, it will create a new command for your command suite named initconfig that will generate the config file (if it doesn't exist), initialized with the values of any options you specify on the command line when calling initconfig.

Let's add this feature to todo and see how it works. First we call config_file:

make_config_easy/todo/bin/todo
```
include GLI
```

➤ ```
config_file File.join(ENV['HOME'],'.todo.rc.yaml')
```

Then we invoke todo using the new initconfig command:

```
$ todo --url=http://jira.example.com --username=davec \
       --password=S3cr3tP@ss initconfig
```

We can then see the config file that was generated:

```
$ cat ~/.todo.rc.yaml
---
:url: http://jira.example.com
:username: davec
:password: S3cr3tP@ss
commands:
  :list:
    :format:
  :new:
    :p:
    :f:
  :done:
```

We can now use todo's new feature without any of the complexity on the command line:

```
$ todo new "Create tables for new analytics"
# => Adds the task to JIRA
```

As an aside, we can see that our short-form-only options make things hard for the user. :p isn't a very clear configuration option; the user will have to get help on the new command to figure out what it does. Compare that to our new global option :username, which states exactly what it is.
```

So far, we've used configuration to control the default values of command-line options. Should configuration control other aspects of our command-line apps? In short, no. We'll explain why in the next section.

6.4 Design Considerations When Using Configuration

We stated that the configuration files for our command-line apps should not contain any configuration beyond default values for command-line options. This may sound limiting, but it's a design constraint that will lead us to make our applications better.

Suppose we wanted to allow a power user to configure the level of compression that gzip uses. gzip takes an option of the form -# where # can be any number from 1 to 9, with 1 indicating a fast but weaker compression and with 9 being a slower but better compression. We might be tempted to put this in our configuration file:

```
---
:force: true
:username: admin
:password: Sup3rS3cret!
:compression: 1

if options[:gzip]
  gzip_command = "gzip"
  if options[:compression]
    gzip_command += " -#{options[:compression]}"
  end
  # run gzip using gzip_command
end
```

Why should this option be limited to just users of the configuration file? Why not make it a full-fledged command-line option, available to anyone? We can easily signify it as an "advanced" option by using only a long-form name like --compression.

You should start to think of your command-line options as the *only* way to affect the behavior of your app. With sensible defaults and the ability to read in external configuration, it won't ultimately matter how many options your app takes. Think of the configuration file as nothing more than a way to specify defaults for the command-line options. This leads to a very clear and easy-to-understand application design principle: give users the power to control and script the entire application at the command line, but provide a configuration file to allow anyone to override them.

6.5 Moving On

In this chapter, we learned how to make our applications configurable so that they can be easy to use for as many users as possible. We saw that driving our application design around command-line arguments and making *those* the vocabulary of our configuration can result in a clean, comprehensible application.

Everything we've learned up to this point has been to get our apps running well and ready for use by others. What we haven't talked about is how to get our app into the hands of its users. This is what we'll talk about next: making it painless for our users to install our apps.

Distribute Painlessly

For our apps to achieve their full potential, we need to get them into the hands of users. In this chapter, we'll learn how to distribute our apps to both users and developers.

We'll start by learning about RubyGems, Ruby's standard deployment mechanism. We'll see how to use RubyGems for public and private distribution. After that, we'll learn how to deploy our apps in environments that are more tightly controlled, where RubyGems is not available. Finally, we'll see how to set up our codebase so that we can distribute our code to other developers and work more collaboratively on our apps.

7.1 Distributing with RubyGems

RubyGems is the standard way to distribute Ruby apps and libraries; if you have written a Rails app or done any nontrivial Ruby programming, you've likely used the gem command to install third-party code onto your system. We used it earlier to install libraries like gli and ronn. RubyGems is designed to make it very simple to install Ruby code, and this includes command-line applications. For example, rake, the standard Ruby build tool, can be installed via RubyGems like so:

```
$ sudo gem install rake
Installing rake 0.8.7.......
$ rake -V
rake, version 0.8.7
```

In addition to painlessly installing and updating Ruby applications, RubyGems is also used to install an app's dependencies. Suppose, for example, our app parses XML; we might use the popular Nokogiri library to handle it. We can indicate to RubyGems that our app requires Nokogiri, and RubyGems will install it when someone installs our app (unless it's already installed).

To configure our application for installation by RubyGems, we need to do three things: create a gem specification, package our code as a gem file, and make it available via a gem server.

Creating a Gem Specification

A gem's specification is a piece of Ruby code called a *gemspec*. This file needs to be created only once and needs to be changed only if we change things about our app, such as the files or list of authors.

A gemspec is exactly what it sounds like: a spec for creating a gem. Essentially, it's a chunk of Ruby code that the gem command will read and execute to understand our app, such as its name, files, and dependencies. Your gemspec should be named YOUR_APP.gemspec where YOUR_APP is the name of your app's executable (which should be all lowercase). The file should be located in the root directory of your project. Here's a sample gemspec we might use for todo, our task-management app:

```ruby
Gem::Specification.new do |s|
  s.name        = "todo"
  s.version     = "0.0.1"
  s.platform    = Gem::Platform::RUBY
  s.authors     = ["David Copeland"]
  s.email       = ["davec at naildrivin5.com"]
  s.homepage    = "http://www.naildrivin5.com/todo"
  s.summary     = %q{A lightweight task-management app}
  s.description = %q{Todo allows you to manage and prioritize
                     tasks on the command line}

  s.rubyforge_project = "todo"

  s.files       = ["bin/todo"]
  s.executables = ["bin/todo"]
  s.add_dependency("gli")
end
```

Ideally, the fields in the gemspec are self-explanatory, but it's worth calling out a few of the fields that are most important.

files
    This is a list of the files that will be part of your gem. It's important that this list is correct, or your gem won't work when installed.

executables
    This is the name of your app's executable. By specifying this, RubyGems will set up your app in the user's path when it's installed.

add_dependency

> Each call to add_dependency will indicate a dependency on a third-party gem. For example, in the gemspec for todo, we've indicated that our app needs GLI. When the user installs todo, RubyGems will see the dependency on GLI and install it.

Much of this information, such as the name of our app and its description, is static; it won't change very often. Some of the information, however, might change more frequently, such as the filename and the version number. We'd like this to be derived. For example, we might store our app's version in a constant so it can be printed in the help text. Since our gemspec is just Ruby code, we can access this constant and use it, rather than duplicating the value.

Let's assume that a file lib/todo_version.rb exists and contains the version number of our app:

install_remove/todo/lib/todo_version.rb

```
module Todo
  VERSION = '0.0.1'
end
```

Since our gemspec is Ruby code, we can use require to import that file and access the VERSION constant:

```
➤ $LOAD_PATH.push File.expand_path("../lib", __FILE__)
➤ require "todo_version"

  Gem::Specification.new do |s|
    s.name       = "todo"
➤   s.version    = Todo::VERSION
    s.platform   = Gem::Platform::RUBY
```

$LOAD_PATH is the variable that holds Ruby's load path, which is where Ruby looks for files when we require them. We add the path to the lib directory within our project and then require todo_version.rb.

Now, when we change the version of our app, our gemspec will automatically know about the new version number. If we wanted to get fancy, we could extract the summary information we use in our banner into a similar constant and use that value for the gemspec's summary.

Now that we have a gemspec, we're ready to package our code as a .gem file so we can distribute it.

Packaging Code in a Gem File

Gems are created with the gem command, which we can run directly on the command line. Entering the command can become tiresome, so we're going to use rake to script it. rake is Ruby's build-automation tool, and it's standard practice to automate any build and maintenance tasks in a Rakefile.

The Rakefile should be stored in the root directory of your project, which is also where the gemspec is located. RubyGems provides a rake task you can use in your Rakefile that will package your gem for you, as follows:

```
require 'rake/gempackagetask'

spec = eval(File.read('todo.gemspec'))

Rake::GemPackageTask.new(spec) do |pkg|
end
```

This is all that's needed. If we ask rake to show us the available tasks via rake -T, we can see that we have a task named package available:

```
$ rake -T
rake clobber_package  # Remove package products
rake gem              # Build the gem file todo-0.0.1.gem
rake package          # Build all the packages
rake repackage        # Force a rebuild of the package files
```

To build our gem, we use the package task:

```
$ rake package
mkdir -p pkg
  Successfully built RubyGem
  Name: todo
  Version: 0.0.1
  File: todo-0.0.1.gem
mv todo-0.0.1.gem pkg/todo-0.0.1.gem
```

We can now install our gem locally via the gem command:

```
$ gem install pkg/todo-0.0.1.gem
Successfully installed todo-0.0.1
1 gem installed
Installing ri documentation for todo-0.0.1...
Installing RDoc documentation for todo-0.0.1...
$ todo help
usage: todo [global options] command [command options]

Version: 0.0.1

Global Options:
    -f, --filename=todo_file - Path to the todo file (default: ~/.todo.txt)
```

```
Commands:
    done       - Complete a task
    help       - Shows list of commands or help for one command
    initconfig - Initialize the config file using current global options
    list       - List tasks
    new        - Create a new task in the task list
```

Notice how we can run todo directly without having to explicitly run it out of bin. todo is now an app installed in our path just like any other application.

This method of installing a gem is not typical; users will more often install gems served from a remote gem server. Despite this, it's still a good idea to install your gem manually before distributing it, as a last check to make sure things are working. Once you've done that, you'll need to push your gem to a gem server so others can install it.

Pushing a Gem to a Gem Server

For open source applications, the simplest gem server to use for your apps is the canonical one provided at http://www.rubygems.org. This is where most users will look and is where gem will also look by default when you issue a gem install command. If you are writing internal applications that you don't want distributed as open source, you can run a gem server internally and make a one-time configuration to your local environment to find gems from your internal server. Let's look at the two options.

Distributing Gems via RubyGems.org

To distribute to your app through http://www.rubygems.org, you'll need to create an account there. This is a one-time-only task, and you'll need to provide your login credentials the first time you push a gem to the server.

Next, you'll need to make sure that the name of your gem isn't in use already. Since RubyGems.org is the central repository for almost all open source Ruby code, you may find that the name of your gem is already taken. If your name *is* taken, you should do the following:

- Change your executable's name.
- Change the name of your gemspec file.
- Change the name of your gem in the gemspec.
- Change any modules in your code and rename your source files to match the new name.

This might sound onerous, but we've taken several steps throughout our journey to minimize the impact of such renames (you'll recall in Chapter 3,

Be Helpful, on page 33 that we derived our executable name in our help strings; this is one reason why). Once you're sure your gem name is available, you can use the gem push command to push your gem to the server:

```
$ gem push pkg/todo-0.0.1.gem
Pushing gem to rubygems.org
Successfully registered gem: todo (0.0.1.gem)
```

The first time you push your gem, you'll be asked for your RubyGems.org name and password; gem should store this information for future pushes. Now, you can go onto any other machine where RubyGems is installed and install your app:

```
$ gem install todo
Successfully installed todo-0.0.1
1 gem installed
Installing ri documentation for todo-0.0.1...
Installing RDoc documentation for todo-0.0.1...
```

RubyGems.org is great for open source apps, but for internal apps that you don't want to make available to the rest of the world, you'll need to set up a gem server internally.

Setting Up and Using an Internal Gem Server

Although the code that powers http://www.rubygems.org is open source and you could deploy it on your company's intranet, this is not recommended, because the app is very complex and likely overpowered for your needs. Instead, you can use the much simpler geminabox.[1]

geminabox is incredibly easy to set up and use and allows you to push gems to it for internal distribution, via the inabox command it adds to gem. It also provides a rudimentary web interface to let you browse the installed gems. The first thing you'll need to do is install it:

```
$ gem install geminabox
Fetching: rack-1.3.3.gem (100%)
Fetching: tilt-1.3.3.gem (100%)
Fetching: sinatra-1.2.6.gem (100%)
Fetching: geminabox-0.3.1.gem (100%)
Successfully installed rack-1.3.3
Successfully installed tilt-1.3.3
Successfully installed sinatra-1.2.6
Successfully installed geminabox-0.3.1
4 gems installed
```

---

1. https://github.com/cwninja/geminabox

Next, you'll need to make a directory where your gems will be stored. When you set this up on a real server, you'll want to choose a more appropriate location, but to see how things work, you can serve them right out of your current directory:

```
$ mkdir gems
```

Now, create a small configuration file called config.ru:

```
require "rubygems"
require "geminabox"

Geminabox.data = "gems"
run Geminabox
```

Then, start up the server:

```
$ rackup
[2011-09-18 05:47:33] INFO  WEBrick 1.3.1
[2011-09-18 05:47:33] INFO  ruby 1.8.7 (2011-06-30) [i686-darwin11.0.1]
[2011-09-18 05:47:33] INFO  WEBrick::HTTPServer#start: pid=34947 port=9292
```

If you navigate to http://localhost:9292, you'll see the web interface for geminabox. Although you can upload gems from this interface, we won't use it; we work from the command line, and we want to be able to script it. Open a new shell window and navigate to the todo project. We can push a gem to the server via the inabox command that was added to gem by installing gem inabox. You can build and push your gem as follows:

```
$ rake package
  Successfully built RubyGem
  Name: todo
  Version: 0.0.1
  File: todo-0.0.1.gem
mv todo-0.0.1.gem pkg/todo-0.0.1.gem
$ gem inabox pkg/todo-0.0.1.gem
Pushing todo-0.0.1.gem to http://localhost:9292...
```

The first time you execute gem inabox, gem will ask for the host where the server is running; just enter http://localhost:9292, and it will do the rest. If you navigate to http://localhost:9292 in your browser, you can see that your gem has been received and is ready for installation. To install it, open a new shell window and type the following:

```
$ gem install --source http://localhost:9292 todo
Successfully installed todo-0.0.1
1 gem installed
```

That's all there is to it! You can alleviate the need to use --source every time by executing the one-time command gem sources -a http://localhost:9292. As a final note, geminabox doesn't provide any authentication. Make sure you deploy your server somewhere secure or password-protect it.

We've seen how easy it is use RubyGems for open source as well as internal distribution of our apps, but managing your apps with RubyGems is not always an option. In the next section, we'll see how to achieve a similar style of distribution using tools that might be easier to deploy inside a more controlled environment.

7.2 Distributing Without RubyGems

Many servers are tightly managed, and installing gems via RubyGems is not an option. System administrators of such systems prefer to have a single way of getting code onto the server, using the packaging system provided by the operating system. This complicates our job of making our apps easily deployable. Distributing gems in such environments is hard but not impossible.

To demonstrate how you might do this, we'll walk through packaging our gem as an RPM, which can be used with Red Hat's yum distribution system.

RPM is the package management system used by many Linux distributions such as Red Hat, Fedora, and CentOS. Creating an RPM can be done using gem2rpm.[2] First, install it (this can be done anywhere, not necessarily on the machine where you'll install the RPM):

```
$ gem install gem2rpm
```

Next, get a copy of your gem file. If you have it available in a RubyGems repository, you can simply do the following:

```
$ gem fetch todo
```

This will download the latest version of your gem to the directory where you ran the command. The next step is to create a spec file. This isn't a gemspec but another file that RPM uses to describe and install your gem. gem2rpm will create this spec file for us by running it as follows:

```
$ gem2rpm -o rubygem-todo.spec todo-1.0.0.gem
```

gem2rpm should create the file rubygem-todo.spec in the current directory. Note that the format of the filename is idiomatic; all RubyGem packages for RPM should be named rubygem-GEMNAME without the version information.

---

2. https://github.com/lutter/gem2rpm

If your gem doesn't include native code (such as C extensions), this should be all you need to do. Your next step is to create the actual RPM package using rpmbuild, which should be available wherever RPM is installed. RPM expects a certain directory structure, and if you see the following error message, it's most likely because you don't have it set up correctly.

```
$ rpmbuild -ba rubygem-todo.spec
ERROR:  could not find gem /usr/src/redhat/SOURCES/todo-1.0.0.gem
        locally or in a repository
```

To correct the error, simply copy your .gem file to /usr/src/redhat/SOURCES and rerun the command:

```
> rpmbuild -ba rubygem-todo.spec
# Some output omitted...
Wrote: /usr/src/redhat/RPMS/noarch/rubygem-todo-1.0.0-1.noarch.rpm
```

The RPM for your gem is now located in /usr/src/redhat/RPMS. It can be installed using whatever means your system administrator prefers (e.g., a local RPM server). Note that the RPM created this way is not signed; signing is outside the scope of this book, but for internal distribution, your system administrator shouldn't have a problem installing this RPM package.

Now that we know how to get our apps into the hands of users, it's worth talking about getting them into the hands of other developers. For an open source project, you might want to solicit contributions and bug fixes from the community. For an internal application, you'll likely need to work with other developers, or others might need to maintain your code. In either case, we want other developers to get up to speed with our code as easily as users can install it.

7.3 Collaborating with Other Developers

We've talked a lot about making an awesome command-line app that is easy to use. We also want our application to be easy to develop and maintain. This reduces the burden on us and others for fixing bugs and adding new features (which, in turn, helps our users). This section is all about making sure the initial setup for developers is painless.

To allow developers to get up and running quickly, we need to provide two things: a way to manage development-time dependencies and a way to provide and manage developer documentation. We'll also talk briefly about setting up an open source project on GitHub, which is a great way to allow other developers to contribute to your open source project.

Managing Development Dependencies

Unlike runtime dependencies, which are needed by users of an app, *development dependencies* are needed only by developers. Such dependencies range from testing libraries like RSpec to rake itself. Developers should be able to install all the gems they need with one command and get up and running as easily as possible. This will save you time in documenting the setup and make it easier for developers to contribute.

We can specify these dependencies in the gemspec and manage their installation with Bundler.[3] Bundler was created to help manage the dependencies for Ruby on Rails projects, but it's a general-purpose tool and will work great for us. It's also what most seasoned Rubyists will expect.

First, let's specify our development dependencies. Although rake and RDoc are typically installed with Ruby, their inclusion is not guaranteed, and users might not necessarily have the versions of these tools that we require. Let's add them explicitly as development dependencies to our gemspec by way of add_development_dependency:

```
Gem::Specification.new do |s|
  s.name       = "todo"
  s.version    = "0.0.1"

  # Rest of the gemspec...

  s.add_dependency("gli")
➤ s.add_development_dependency("rake","~> 0.8.7")
➤ s.add_development_dependency("rdoc","~> 3.9.0")
end
```

Now, we need a way for developers to install these dependencies automatically. Bundler does exactly this; will examine our gemspec for the gems and versions and install the correct dependencies. Although we have these dependencies installed already, we want to configure Bundler so other developers can get them installed simply. First we install it with Bundler:

```
$ gem install bundler
Successfully installed bundler-1.0.15
1 gem installed
Installing ri documentation for bundler-1.0.15...
Installing RDoc documentation for bundler-1.0.15...
```

Bundler uses a file named Gemfile to control what it does. For a Rails app, this file would contain all of the gems needed to run the app. Since we've specified

---

3.   http://gembundler.com

them in our gemspec, we can tell Bundler to look there, instead of repeating them in Gemfile. Our Gemfile looks like so:

```
source :rubygems
gemspec
```

This tells Bundler to search the common RubyGems repository for needed gems and to look in the gemspec for the list of which gems are needed and what versions to fetch. If you've set up an internal gem server to host private gems, you can add additional source lines, giving the URL to your server as the argument.

Even though we have all these gems installed already, it's still important to run Bundler, because it will generate an additional file that other developers will need. Let's run it first and then see what it did. This is the same command developers will run to get started working on your app.

```
$ bundle install
Using gli (1.3.2)
Using rake (0.8.7)
Using rdoc (3.9.4)
Using todo (0.0.1) from source at .
Using bundler (1.0.17)
Your bundle is complete! Use `bundle show [gemname]` to see where a bundled
gem is installed.
```

If you were paying close attention, you'll notice that we specified the version 3.9.0 of rdoc as a development deployment, but Bundler installed 3.9.4. What if version 3.9.5 of rdoc is released? When a new developer starts on our app, which version should be installed?

Bundler is designed to allow you to tightly control what versions are installed. When we ran bundle install earlier, it created a file called Gemfile.lock. This file contains the *exact* versions of each gem that was installed. We used the ~> symbol (a tilde, followed by the greater-than symbol) to specify our dependence on rdoc, meaning that any version number with the format 3.9.*x* would be acceptable. Bundler used the latest version that satisfied this dependency.

Suppose rdoc 3.9.5 is released. If we were to check Gemfile.lock into version control and a new developer checked it out and ran bundle install, Bundler would install *3.9.4*, even though 3.9.5 is the latest version that satisfies our development dependency. This allows us to ensure that everyone is using the exact same gem versions that we are.

Now that we have a way to get new developers up and running quickly, we need a way to document anything additional to help them collaborate.

Writing and Generating Documentation

The documentation you provide with your project should be aimed mostly at developers. The in-app help and man page are where you can document things for your users, so you can use RDoc and a README file to get developers up to speed (although you should include a pointer to would-be users in your README as well).

The README is particularly important, since it's the first thing a developer will see when examining your source code. It's the ideal place to include instructions for developers to help understand what your app does and how to work with it.

Your README should be in RDoc format so you can include it when you generate and publish your RDoc. This allows you to connect your overview documentation to your code and API documentation. If you aren't familiar with RDoc, it's a plain-text format, similar to Markdown but geared toward documenting Ruby code. To use it effectively, you need to create a README.rdoc and then add the RDoc task to your Rakefile to automate document generation.

Your README.rdoc should have the following format:

1. Application name and brief description
2. Author list, copyright notice, and license
3. Installation and basic usage instructions for users
4. Instructions for developers

Although the README is primarily developer documentation, it's a good idea to include some brief pointers for users who happen to come across the source code for your app. Everything else in the file should be about helping developers get up to speed. Here's an example of a README.rdoc that we might write for our database backup app, db_backup.rb:

install_remove/db_backup/README.rdoc
```
= `db_backup` - Iteration-aware MySQL database backups

Author::   David Copeland (mailto:dave@example.com)
Copyright:: Copyright (c) 2011 by David Copeland
License:: Distributes under the Apache License,
          see LICENSE.txt in the source distro

This application provides an easy interface to backing up MySQL databases,
using a canonical naming scheme for both daily backups and
"end-of-iteration" backups.

== Install
```

```
Install:

    gem install db_backup

== Use

Backup a database:

    db_backup.rb my_database

For more help:

    db_backup.rb --help
    gem man db_backup.rb

== Developing for `db_backup`

First, install bundler:

    gem install bundler

Get the development dependencies

    bundle install

Most of the code is in `bin/db_backup.rb`.
```

The RDoc format provides most of what you'll need to write good documentation. See RDoc's RDoc[4] for a complete description of the format.

To publish the documentation, we want to create HTML versions of it, which can be done via the RDoc rake task.

install_remove/db_backup/Rakefile
```
require 'rake/rdoctask'

Rake::RDocTask.new do |rd|
  rd.main = "README.rdoc"
  rd.rdoc_files.include("README.rdoc","lib/**/*.rb","bin/**/*")
  rd.title = 'db_backup - Backup MySQL Databases'
end
```

Now, you can generate RDoc via rake as follows:

```
$ rake rdoc
(in /Users/davec/Projects/db_backup)
rm -r html

Generating HTML...
```

---

4.   http://rdoc.sourceforge.net/doc/index.html

```
Files:    3
Classes:  0
Modules:  1
Methods:  0
Elapsed:  0.105s
```

You can then view the RDoc be opening html/index.html in your browser. For an open source app, you'll want to use a service like RDoc.info to publish your RDoc (we'll see how to set that up in the next section). For internal apps, you can simply copy the HTML to a local intranet server.

Managing an Open Source App on GitHub

Although there are many free services to manage open source code, GitHub[5] has become one of the most popular, especially among members of the Ruby community. Hosting your open source project here will expose it to a large audience of active developers.

Although GitHub has many resources of its own to get you started, we'll go over a few points here that will help you successfully manage your open source app. To get started, first go to GitHub and perform the following steps:

1. Create your account on GitHub.

2. Create a new open source project under your account (this is completely free).

3. Import your repository (GitHub includes very clear and specific instructions on doing this, which we won't re-create here).

Make sure that the name you choose for your repository matches the name of your app (which should match the gem name you chose as well). Once you've imported your project, you'll note that GitHub helpfully renders your README.rdoc as HTML. This is another great reason to have a README.

GitHub includes an issue-tracking system and a wiki. If these tools are helpful to you, by all means use them, but the feature you'll definitely want to set up is called *service hooks*. These hooks allow you to connect web services to your commits. Of greatest interest to us is the hook for RDocinfo. http://rdoc.info is a free service that will generate and host your project's RDoc. The HTML version of your RDoc will be generated every time you commit. This is a great alternative to hosing it yourself, and it's very easy to set up in GitHub. Here are the steps:

---

5.   http://www.github.com

1. Navigate in your browser to your project's GitHub page.

2. Click the Admin button, and then click the Service Hooks link.

3. Scroll down until you see the link for RDocinfo and click it.

4. Scroll back up and check the box to activate it, followed by clicking the Update Settings button.

5. Now, make a change to your project's code, commit that change, and push it up to GitHub.

The service hook should kick in, and your project's RDoc will be available at *http://rubydoc.info/github/your-name/your-project*, where "your-name" is your GitHub username and "your-project" is the name of your project. If you set your project's URL to this one, developers will have a very easy time finding your documentation and development instructions, making it a snap for them to contribute!

7.4 Moving On

You now know everything you need to get your app into the hands of both users and developers. Whether you are working on an open source project to share with the world or an internal app for the exclusive use of your company, RubyGems, and various tools related to it, have you covered.

At this point, we can conceive, build, and distribute an awesome command-line application. But, what happens now? Once users start using your app, they're sure to find bugs, and they'll definitely want new features. We've taken a lot of steps to make it easy on ourselves to respond to our users, but there's more that we can be doing, especially as our apps become more complex and featureful.

The best way to quickly respond to our users and maintain the level of quality and polish we've put into our app is to have a test suite—a way to verify that our app does what we say it does and to check that it doesn't break when we make changes. Ideally, we would've started off this book with a discussion of tests, but we wanted to focus first on the principles and tools you need to build awesome apps. Now it's time to look at testing, which we'll do in the next chapter. When it comes to testing, command-line apps present their own challenges, but, as usual, the Ruby ecosystem of libraries and open source projects will help us overcome them.

Test, Test, Test

Writing perfect code isn't easy. It might even be impossible. That's why seasoned developers—including command-line application developers—write tests. Tests are the best tool we have to make sure our applications perform flawlessly, and the Ruby community is especially friendly to testing, thanks to the culture and tools established by Ruby on Rails.

Command-line applications often interact with various systems and environments, which produces a unique set of challenges for testing. If you've done any web application development, you are probably accustomed to having different "tiers," such as a development tier and a testing tier. These tiers are complete systems, often using many servers to provide an environment for isolated testing. This is impractical for command-line apps, so we tend to develop command-line apps on the system where they are intended to run. Therefore, if we wanted to test adding a task to our task list using todo, it would add a task to our actual task list, if we didn't take steps to keep it from doing so.

What we'll learn here is how to write and run tests for our command-line apps, as well as some techniques to keep our tests from causing problems on our system. We'll do this by combining two types of tests: unit tests and acceptance tests. You are probably familiar with unit testing, which is useful in testing the small bits of logic that comprise our application. Ruby's standard library includes all the tools we'll need.

Acceptance testing takes the opposite approach. Acceptance tests simulate real user behavior and exercise the entire system. We'll learn about this type of testing by using the popular Cucumber testing tool, along with Aruba, which is an extension to Cucumber designed to help test command-line applications. Acceptance tests are a good place to start because of the user-centered approach, so let's jump in and see how they work. After we have a good set of acceptance tests, we'll turn our attention to unit tests to test edge cases that might be hard to simulate using acceptance tests.

8.1 Testing User Behavior with Acceptance Tests

Unlike web applications, command-line apps have simple user interfaces, and their output is less complex. This makes the job of simulating input and testing output relatively simple. The problems come in when we consider what our apps do. db_backup.rb takes a long time to do its work and requires access to a database. todo makes irreversible changes to its task list. We need a way to run our apps that mimics as closely as possible the "real-world" scenarios they were written to solve but in a repeatable and predictable way that doesn't cause permanent changes to our environment.

Rather than solve this problem at the same we learn about the mechanics of testing, let's take things one step at a time. If you recall, todo takes a global option that controls where the task list is. We can use that to keep our tests from messing with our personal task list in our home directory. Let's use that to get some tests going. After we see how to test our app in general, we'll discuss some techniques to deal with the "tests messing with our personal task list" issue.

Understanding Acceptance Tests

Acceptance tests are tests that we can use to confirm that an app properly implements certain features, from a user's perspective. Acceptance tests typically test only the subset of the actions users are likely to attempt (the so-called happy path), and they don't cover uncommon edge cases. What acceptance tests should do is to simulate the ways users are most likely to employ our tool to do their job. A todo user, for example, is likely to do the following:

- Add a new task
- List tasks
- Complete a task
- Get help

Each task maps to a command that todo accepts. To test these, we need to use todo just as a user would. We can also use todo to verify its own behavior. For example, we can execute a todo list, capture the list of tasks, add a new task via todo new, and then list the tasks again, this time looking for our new task. We could use the same technique to test todo done.

While we could create *another* command-line app to run these tests, we don't need to do so. The acceptance testing tool Cucumber (explained in great detail in *The RSpec Book* [CADH09]) can handle the basic infrastructure for running tests, and the Cucumber add-on library Aruba will provide us with the tools we need to run our app and verify its behavior. First we'll see how these tools work, then we'll set them up, and finally we'll write our tests.

Understanding Cucumber and Aruba

Acceptance tests written in Cucumber don't look like the tests you might be used to seeing. They're written in what looks like plain English.[1] With Cucumber, you describe the behavior you want to test, in English, and then write code that runs under the covers to execute the procedure you have specified.

Now, you can't just write free-form text; there *is* a structure that you'll need to follow to make this work. Cucumber delineates tests into *features*, which contain multiple *scenarios*. A feature is what it sounds like: a feature of your application. "Adding a task" is a feature. A scenario exercises an aspect of a feature. For example, we might have a scenario to add a task to an existing task list and another to add a task for the very first time.

In Cucumber, you describe the feature in free-form English; this part of the test is mere documentation. The scenarios, however, must follow a strict format. Each scenario has a one-line description and is followed by *steps*. Steps start with "Given," "When," "Then," "And," or "But," for example "Given the file /tmp/todo.txt exists" or "Then the output should contain Hello." These steps are what Cucumber will actually execute to run your test. Before we get into the weeds of how this works under the covers, let's look at a simple feature and scenario for todo:

```
tolerate_gracefully/todo/features/todo.feature
Feature: We can add new tasks
  As a busy developer with a lot of things to do
  I want to keep a list of tasks I need to work on

Scenario: Add a new task
  Given the file "/tmp/todo.txt" doesn't exist
  When I successfully run `todo -f /tmp/todo.txt new 'Some new task'`
  Then I successfully run `todo -f /tmp/todo.txt list`
  And the stdout should contain "Some new task"
```

---

1. Cucumber supports other human languages as well, from Arabic to Vietnamese.

As you can see, we've followed Cucumber's particular format, but the test is written in plain English. You could take these instructions and manually execute them on the command line to check that adding a task works correctly.

Seeing the text of this test gives us some insight as to the use of "Given," "When," and "Then." These three words help to differentiate the three main parts of any good test: setup, action, and verification. More precisely:

Given

> This sets up the conditions of the test. Most tests operate under a set of assumptions, and each "Given" step establishes what those are. In our case, we are establishing that the task list doesn't exist so that when we later add a task to it, we can be sure that our action had an effect (if we didn't have this bit of setup, a tasklist might exist that contains the task we're adding, resulting in our test always passing, even if our app was broken).

When

> This performs the action or actions under test. In our case, we run todo new to, ideally, add a new task.

Then

> This verifies that our action taken in a "When" had the desired outcome. For our earlier scenario, we verify that todo new worked by running todo list and examining its output.

And or But

> These two words can be used anywhere and "extend" the keyword they follow. We're using that in our "Then" section, because we need two steps to perform a full verification. The use of "And" over "But" is purely cosmetic; use whatever "reads" the best to you.

Back to our scenario, we now have a set of steps that, as we mentioned, we could manually execute to test our app. Of course, we don't want to have to run our tests manually; we're using Cucumber to automate all of this, so let's dig a bit deeper to see how Cucumber can run this test. We'll get into the specifics of where files go and what their names are, so for now, let's assume that we can ask Cucumber to run this feature for us.

The first step of our scenario is Given the file "/tmp/todo.txt" doesn't exist. This is a setup step that ensures we don't have a tasklist sitting around from a previous test run that might already have our about-to-be-added task in it. Cucumber doesn't know how to perform this setup step, so we need to give it the code to do so. We'll define the step using the method Given, provided by Cucumber, that takes a regexp and a block. If the text of our step matches that regexp, the block is executed. Let's see this step's definition:

```
tolerate_gracefully/todo/features/step_definitions/cli_steps.rb
Given /^the file "([^"]*)" doesn't exist$/ do |file|
  FileUtils.rm(file) if File.exists? file
end
```

You'll notice that the regexp has a capture in it (this part: ([^"]*)). Cucumber will extract whatever matched that capture and provide it as an argument to our block. This means we could write another step, Given the file "/tmp/some_other_file.txt" doesn't exist, and this step definition would work for it, too. Using this technique, you could build up a library of reusable step definitions. This is exactly what Aruba is: a set of general-purpose step definitions for writing scenarios to test command-line apps.

The next two steps of our scenario, both of the form "I successfully run 'some command,'" are defined by Aruba, meaning we don't have to provide step definitions for those steps. This also demonstrates an interesting aspect of Cucumber. At a code level, Given, When, Then, And, and But are all treated the same. We could have every step start with "And" and Cucumber wouldn't care; these keywords are for human eyes, not the computer. Further, when we define steps, Cucumber provides Given, When, and Then to do so, but the effect is the same regardless of which one we use. This is how we're able to use the same step as both a "When" and a "Then."

Coming back to the Aruba-provided step "I successfully run 'some command,'" this does two things: it executes the command in the backticks, and it checks its exit status. If it's zero, the test will proceed. If it's nonzero, the test will halt with a failure (there is a less stringent version provided, "I run 'some_command,'" that will just run the command and not check the exit status). The final step is also defined by Aruba and allows us to assert that the standard output of our app's run contains a particular string.

Now that you have an idea of what Cucumber is and a general sense of how it works, let's actually get it set up for our project so we can run this feature.

Installing and Setting Up Cucumber and Aruba

To install Cucumber and Aruba, we need only add the aruba gem to our gemspec (as a development dependency; our app doesn't require aruba to run). Because Aruba depends on Cucumber, when you update your gems with Bundler, Cucumber will be installed automatically (see the note on Windows at *Using Aruba on Windows*, on page 122). Here's the updated gemspec:

Using Aruba on Windows

As of this writing, Aruba does not work "out of the box" on Windows. Discussions on the Internet involve varying degrees of functionality, but there doesn't seem to be a strong consensus that Aruba works on Windows.

If you are adventurous, I encourage you to attempt to get the Cucumber tests in this section passing on Windows and submit a patch. Windows is an important operating system for the Ruby community that is, currently, sorely underrepresented in compatibility. This particular application, spawning processes and monitoring their behavior, is particularly tricky, because of the large differences between UNIX and Windows. Since OS X is based on UNIX, Macs tend to work just fine.

I still encourage you to follow along with this section, because it will teach you solid principles on acceptance testing your apps; you may need to take a different approach until Aruba is more compatible with Windows.

---

tolerate_gracefully/todo/todo.gemspec

```ruby
spec = Gem::Specification.new do |s|
  s.name = 'todo'
  s.version = Todo::VERSION
  # rest of the gemspec...

  s.bindir = 'bin'
  s.executables << 'todo'
  s.add_development_dependency('aruba', '~> 0.4.6')
  s.add_dependency('gli')
end
```

Now, we tell Bundler to make sure our development dependencies are up-to-date:

```
$ bundle install
Using ffi (1.0.9)
Using childprocess (0.1.9)
Using builder (3.0.0)
Using diff-lcs (1.1.2)
Using json (1.5.1)
Using gherkin (2.4.0)
Using term-ansicolor (1.0.5)
Using cucumber (0.10.6)
Using rspec-core (2.6.4)
Using rspec-expectations (2.6.0)
Using rspec-mocks (2.6.0)
Using rspec (2.6.0)
Using aruba (0.3.7)
Using gli (1.3.2)
Using todo (0.0.1) from source at .
Using bundler (1.0.17)
```

Cucumber has a conventional file structure where the directory features (off of the project's root directory) contains the .feature files containing our scenarios. Inside that directory, the directory step_definitions contains the Ruby code to define our steps. The names of the files don't matter; everything with an .rb extension will be loaded. Finally, any Cucumber configuration goes in support/env.rb. We'll see what this file is for later.

Finally, we need to add a task to our Rakefile to allow us to run the Cucumber scenarios:

tolerate_gracefully/todo/Rakefile
```
require 'cucumber'
require 'cucumber/rake/task'

Cucumber::Rake::Task.new(:features) do |t|
  t.cucumber_opts = "features --format pretty -x"
  t.fork = false
end
```

Now that we've seen what our tests look like, implemented the needed steps, and installed all the software we need, let's run our tests.

Running Cucumber Tests

The task we added to our Rakefile creates a task named "features" that will run our Cucumber tests. Let's run it now:

```
$ rake features
Feature: We can add new tasks
  As a busy developer with a lot of things to do
  I want to keep a list of tasks I need to work on

  Scenario: Add a new task
    Given the file "/tmp/todo.txt" doesn't exist
    When I successfully run
      `todo --filename=/tmp/todo.txt new 'Some new todo item'`
    And I successfully run `todo --filename=/tmp/todo.txt list`
    Then the stdout should contain "Some new todo item"
1 scenarios (1 passed)
4 steps (4 passed)
0m0.563s
```

If you're running this locally, you'll notice that the output is green. This means that everything is working and our test passed. Let's introduce a bug to see what happens when our tests fail. Here's our original, correct, CSV formatting code that we saw in Chapter 4, *Play Well with Others*, on page 53:

```
play_well/todo/bin/todo
```
```
complete_flag = completed ? "C" : "U"
printf("%d,%s,%s,%s,%s\n",index,name,complete_flag,created,completed)
```

We'll uppercase the name of the task in our CSV output, which should cause
our test to fail, like so:

```
elsif options[:format] == 'csv'
  # Use the machine-readable CSV format
  complete_flag = completed ? "C" : "U"
➤ printf("%d,%s,%s,%s,%s\n",index,name.upcase,complete_flag,created,completed)
end
```

Now, when we run our feature, one of the steps in our scenario fails:

```
$ rake features
Scenario: Add a new task
  Given the file "/tmp/todo.txt" doesn't exist
  When I successfully run
    `todo --filename=/tmp/todo.txt new 'Some new todo item'`
  And I successfully run `todo --filename=/tmp/todo.txt list`
  Then the stdout should contain "Some new todo item"
  expected "1,SOME NEW TODO ITEM,U,Thu Sep 22 08:44:02 -0400 2011,\n"
    to include "Some new todo item"
  Diff:
  @@ -1,2 +1,2 @@
  -Some new todo item
  +1,SOME NEW TODO ITEM,U,Thu Sep 22 08:44:02 -0400 2011,
   (RSpec::Expectations::ExpectationNotMetError)
  features/todo.feature:17:in `Then the stdout should
      contain "Some new todo item"'

Failing Scenarios:
cucumber features/todo.feature:13 # Scenario: Add a new task

1 scenarios (1 failed)
4 steps (1 failed, 3 passed)
0m0.576s
rake aborted!
Cucumber failed
```

If you're running this locally, all of the error text will be displayed in red,
giving a clear indication that something is wrong. If you look closely, you'll
notice that Aruba has provided us with a diff of the expected output and
received output, making it fairly easy to see the problem that caused our test
to fail.

Testing Complex Behavior

Now that we have a basic path tested, let's see how to test something a bit trickier: the default location of the task list. In our previous scenario, we used the --filename option to explicitly control where todo looked for the task list. This is important, because we don't want our tests to mess with our actual task list, which lives in our home directory. Nevertheless, we *do* need to test that todo correctly uses the task list in our home directory by default. This presents us with a problem.

Testing db_backup.rb presents a similar problem; we need a real database to back up, and backing up a database potentially takes a long time. These are two examples of the challenges we face when testing command-line apps. There's no silver bullet to solve these, but if we think creatively, we can handle most of them. To gain insight into how to approach problems like this in the future, let's write tests for both todo's task list defaulting to our home directory and db_backup.rb backing up a real database.

Testing Access to the Home Directory

It's great that we have the --filename flag to todo; we can get a lot of test coverage without worrying about files in our actual home directory. We *do* need to verify that the default location for the task list gets used. How can we do this without having our tests modify our actual task list?

First let's write the scenario to test what we want and work from there.

```
tolerate_gracefully/todo/features/todo.feature
Scenario: The task list is in our home directory by default
  Given there is no task list in my home directory
  When I successfully run `todo new 'Some new todo item'`
  Then the task list should exist in my home directory
  When I successfully run `todo list`
  Then the stdout should contain "Some new todo item"
```

This should be a good test of the default location; we omit the --filename options, check that a file exists in our home directory, and then use the list command to make sure we're reading from the right place. Before we see how to keep our home directory safe from our tests, let's define all of our steps.

There are two steps in this scenario that we don't have defined. We have steps similar to them; we've implemented the file "xxx" doesn't exist, and Aruba provides the step a file named "xxx" should exist. We can use these steps when making our own, like so:

tolerate_gracefully/todo/features/step_definitions/cli_steps.rb

```
Given /^there is no task list in my home directory$/ do
  step %(the file "#{ENV['HOME']}/.todo.txt" doesn't exist)
end

Then /^the task list should exist in my home directory$/ do
  step %(a file named "#{ENV['HOME']}/.todo.txt" should exist)
end
```

You'll note that we're using ENV['HOME'], which is how we access the HOME environment variable. The system sets this variable to the user's home directory (even on Windows). Assuming that our app uses this to access the user's home directory, we can change its value to another directory that we control. Our tests and the app are still accessing "the user's home directory" in a canonical way, but we can control the contents of that location.

Since apps that Aruba runs inherit the environment of the tests, all we need to do is modify the value of ENV['HOME'] before our scenario runs (and restore its correct value after the scenario exits). Cucumber provides hooks to do just that. The methods Before and After both accept blocks that will execute before and after (respectively) every scenario.

tolerate_gracefully/todo/features/support/env.rb

```
Before do
  @real_home = ENV['HOME']
  fake_home = File.join('/tmp','fake_home')
  FileUtils.rm_rf fake_home, :secure => true
  ENV['HOME'] = fake_home
end
After do
  ENV['HOME'] = @real_home
end
```

As you can see, we create a fresh, empty directory and point ENV['HOME'] to it. Our app uses that same variable like so:

tolerate_gracefully/todo/bin/todo

```
desc "Path to the todo file"
arg_name "todo_file"
➤ default_value File.join(ENV['HOME'],'.todo.txt')
flag [:f,:filename]
```

So, we're able to verify the logic of the task list defaulting to our home directory, without actually using our home directory. Since the location of the "home directory" is really just shorthand for "whatever directory is in ENV['HOME']," we now have test coverage without worrying that our personal task list will be touched. Let's run our new test and make sure it passes. To prove that we aren't touching our home directory, we'll list our actual task list before and after running our feature.

```
$ todo list
1 - Design database schema
    Created:    Sun Oct 02 08:06:12 -0500 2011
2 - Get access to production logs
    Created:    Sun Oct 02 08:06:12 -0500 2011
3 - Code Review
    Created:    Sun Oct 02 08:06:12 -0500 2011
$ rake features
Feature: We can add new tasks
  As a busy developer with a lot of things to do
  I want to keep a list of tasks I need to work on

  Scenario: The task list is in our home directory by default
    Given there is no task list in my home directory
    When I successfully run `todo new 'Some new todo item'`
    Then the task list should exist in my home directory
    When I successfully run `todo list`
    Then the stdout should contain "Some new todo item"

1 scenarios (1 passed)
5 steps (5 passed)
0m0.793s
$ todo list
1 - Design database schema
    Created:    Sun Oct 02 08:06:12 -0500 2011
2 - Get access to production logs
    Created:    Sun Oct 02 08:06:12 -0500 2011
3 - Code Review
    Created:    Sun Oct 02 08:06:12 -0500 2011
```

Our test passed, but our task list wasn't modified—everything worked!

Manipulating the environment is a great technique for testing behavior like this; the environment works as a "middleman" that allows us to change things (like the location of the user's home directory) without affecting the code of our tests or our app. What about testing that certain external commands were called, as in the case of db_backup.rb?

Testing Execution of External Commands

db_backup.rb is basically a specialized wrapper around mysqldump. If we ran db_backup.rb from a Cucumber test as is, it would require a live database and would perform an actual backup. This could be a problem, especially if we ask it to back up a particularly large database.

We could use environment variables again, by setting a special variable that tells db_backup.rb to not actually call mysqldump but instead just print out the command it would normally run.

```
def run(command,exit_on_error_with)
  puts "Running '#{command}'"
  unless ENV['DONT_RUN']
    stdout_str, stderr_str, status = Open3.capture3(command)
    puts stdout_str
    unless status.success?
      STDERR.puts "There was a problem running '#{command}'"
      STDERR.puts stderr_str
      exit exit_on_error_with
    end
  end
end
```

This isn't a very good technique; we want to test that we're calling mysqldump appropriately, and doing something like this skips it entirely. We really should test the entire system from end to end.

An acceptance test of the complete system will give you the best idea of how the app will behave in the hands of users. It's also the most difficult to set up, since it requires a completely controlled testing environment. For the purposes of db_backup.rb, we can set up a database for testing, populate it with a small amount of data, and then run our app, checking that it did what we expected.

First let's write out our scenarios. In this case, we'll run two tests: one for the normal use (where the backup is compressed) and one where we do not compress the backup.

```
tolerate_gracefully/db_backup/features/system_test.feature
Scenario: End-to-end test using a real database
  Given the database backup_test exists
  When I successfully run `db_backup.rb --force -u root backup_test`
  Then the backup file should be gzipped

Scenario: End-to-end test using a real database, skipping gzip
  Given the database backup_test exists
  When I successfully run `db_backup.rb --force -u root --no-gzip backup_test`
  Then the backup file should NOT be gzipped
```

This should look familiar by now. As we've seen, Aruba provides the second step of these scenarios for us, but the rest we have to define. First we'll define our "Given," which sets the stage for our test. We need to set up an entire database in MySQL with *some* data in it. To do that, we'll create a .sql file that will set up our database, create a table, and insert some data:

tolerate_gracefully/db_backup/setup_test.sql

```
drop database if exists backup_test;
create database backup_test;
use backup_test;

create table test_table(
    id int,
    name varchar(255)
);

insert into test_table(id,name) values (1,'Dave'), (2, 'Amy'), (3,'Rudy');
```

We include that in our project and can now reference it in our step definition, which looks like so:

tolerate_gracefully/db_backup/features/step_definitions/system_test_steps.rb

```
MYSQL   = ENV['DB_BACKUP_MYSQL'] || '/usr/local/mysql/bin/mysql'
USER    = ENV['DB_BACKUP_USER'] || 'root'

Given /^the database backup_test exists$/ do
  test_sql_file  = File.join(File.dirname(__FILE__),'..','..','setup_test.sql')
  command = "#{MYSQL} -u#{USER} < #{test_sql_file}"
  stdout,stderr,status = Open3.capture3(command)
  unless status.success?
    raise "Problem running #{command}, stderr was:\n#{stderr}"
  end

end
```

The first two lines set up some defaults for how we're going to run mysql to load the database. In our case, we set the location of the mysql executable and the username we'd like to use when loading the data. We allow this to be overridden via an environment variable so that other developers who might have a different setup can run these tests. This shows some of the complication involved in doing true end-to-end tests. These environment variables should *definitely* be documented in our README file.

Next, we need to define the steps for our two "Thens" (that the backup file should, or should not, be gzipped). To do that, we'll construct the filename we expect db_backup.rb to output, using a .gzip extension or not, depending on the test. Since the filename will contain the current date, we'll need to construct the filename dynamically:

tolerate_gracefully/db_backup/features/step_definitions/system_test_steps.rb

```
def expected_filename
  now = Time.now
  sprintf("backup_test-%4d-%02d-%02d.sql",now.year,now.month,now.day)
end
```

```
Then /^the backup file should be gzipped$/ do
  step %(a file named "#{expected_filename}.gz" should exist)
end

Then /^the backup file should NOT be gzipped$/ do
  now = Time.now
  step %(a file named "#{expected_filename}" should exist)
end
```

Using the expected_filename method, we can defer to an Aruba-provided step a file named "xxx" should exist to perform the actual check. Now, when we run our tests, everything passes:

```
$ rake features
Feature: Do a complete system test

  Scenario: End-to-end test using a real database
    Given the database backup_test exists
    When I successfully run `db_backup.rb --force -u root backup_test`
    Then the backup file should be gzipped

  Scenario: End-to-end test using a real database, skipping gzip
    Given the database backup_test exists
    When I successfully run `db_backup.rb --force -u root --no-gzip backup_test`
    Then the backup file should NOT be gzipped

2 scenarios (2 passed)
6 steps (6 passed)
0m0.745s
```

It's good to be able to actually run our apps in the exact way a user would; however, it's not always going to be possible. Even for something as simple to set up as db_backup.rb, it's still difficult. Another developer will need to set up a MySQL database and make sure it's running, just to run our tests.

You may be creating an even more complex app that interacts with other systems. If you can't figure out a way to set up a good test environment with Aruba, it's still worth writing the automated test but keeping it out of the list of features you run regularly. (Setting this up can be done with the "tags" feature of Cucumber. The documentation[2] should be able to get you started.) Whenever you are ready to release a new version or just want to do a full system test, you can manually set up the proper conditions and have Cucumber run your system test. It's not ideal, but it works for complex apps that can't easily be tested like this.

---

2.   https://github.com/cucumber/cucumber/wiki/Tags

Everything we've talked about up to now has focused on testing our command-line apps by running them the way a user would. This gives us a clear picture of how an app is supposed to work, and we could even use our Cucumber features as supplemental documentation! Where the use of Cucumber starts to break down is when we need to test edge cases. Consider todo. What if the to-do list isn't formatted correctly? What if the task list file isn't writable when we add a new task? What would the app do? What *should* it do?

We went through a fair amount of effort faking out our home directory in testing todo (not to mention the effort we went to in order to test db_backup.rb!). It's going to be even more difficult to set up the conditions that simulate every edge case; it may not even be possible. We still want to test these edge cases, but we aren't going to be able to do it at the acceptance test level using Cucumber. We need to break down our code into smaller, testable units. When we do that, we can test bits of logic in isolation and can more easily simulate some strange error conditions simply in code. These types of tests are called *unit tests*.

8.2   Testing in Isolation with Unit Tests

In addition to allowing greater flexibility in simulating edge cases, unit tests have two other advantages: they run very quickly, since they don't require any setup outside of Ruby (such as files, databases, and so on), and they force us to organize our code into small, testable units. Faster tests are good, since we can more quickly see the health of our app and more quickly and frequently run tests when writing new features and fixing bugs. Having small testable units is good, too, because it means our app will be easier to under-stand and maintain; instead of a big long block of code, we'll have small units that do simple things, all glued together to form the app.

To run unit tests, we'll need to break our code into units that can be tested. Since we have a few tests in place via Cucumber, we'll have some assurance that the code changes we're about to make didn't break anything. This process is called *refactoring* and is very difficult to do without a suite of tests. Let's focus on todo and extract code out of bin/todo and into some files in lib that bin/todo can include. Our soon-to-be-created unit tests can then include these files for testing without having to execute todo.

Extracting Units from Existing Code

The source code for todo is organized around the GLI command methods and blocks. Each action block contains the core logic of our to-do app. This is the logic we need to extract so our unit tests can execute it. Here's the action block for the new command:

```
tolerate_gracefully/todo/bin/todo
c.action do |global_options,options,task_names|
  File.open(global_options[:filename],'a+') do |todo_file|
    if task_names.empty?
      puts "Reading new tasks from stdin..."
      task_names = STDIN.readlines.map { |a| a.chomp }
    end
    tasks = 0
    task_names.each do |task|
      todo_file.puts [task,Time.now].join(',')
      tasks += 1
    end
    if tasks == 0
      raise "You must provide tasks on the command-line or standard input"
    end
  end
end
```

Since Ruby is an object-oriented language, it makes sense to put the code currently in the action block into a class or module and then use it inside the action block. Ultimately, we'd want a class named Task that handled all things task-related, but let's take things one step at a time. All we need is to move the code out of our executable, so we'll create a module named Todo and create a method called new_task inside it. new_task will be a straight copy of the code from our action block:

```
tolerate_gracefully/todo_unit_tests/lib/todo/todo.rb
module Todo
  def new_task(filename,task_names)
    File.open(filename,'a+') do |todo_file|
      tasks = 0
      task_names.each do |task|
        todo_file.puts [task,Time.now].join(',')
        tasks += 1
      end
      if tasks == 0
        raise "You must provide tasks on the command-line or standard input"
      end
    end
  end
end
```

In Ruby, a module can be used for many things, but here, we're using it as a place where code can live that isn't naturally part of a class. Later in the book, we'll make a proper class and have a better OO design for todo, but for now, a module will accomplish our goal of unit testing this code.

Next, we need to remove this code from bin/todo, require lib/todo/todo.rb, and include the Todo module so we can access our new_task method.

```
➤ $LOAD_PATH << File.expand_path(File.dirname(__FILE__) + '/../lib')
  require 'rubygems'
  require 'gli'
  require 'todo_version'
➤ require 'todo/todo.rb'

➤ include Todo
```

The first highlighted line isn't new (GLI included it for us when we first generated our project), but it's worth pointing out because this is how bin/todo will be able to access our newly extracted code that lives in lib/todo/task.rb. All we're doing is placing our lib directory into the load path (accessible in Ruby via $LOAD_PATH).

The next highlighted line requires our code, while the following includes into the current context. This means that any method defined in the Todo module is now available directly for use in our code. Now we can use it in the action block for the new command:

```
  c.action do |global_options,options,task_names|
    if task_names.empty?
      puts "Reading new tasks from stdin..."
      task_names = STDIN.readlines.map { |a| a.chomp }
    end
➤   new_task(global_options[:filename],task_names)
```

When we run our Cucumber tests via rake features, we'll see that all the tests are still green (and thus still passing). This means that our app is still working in light of this fairly major change in its structure. Now, we can start testing this code.

Setting Up Our Environment to Run Unit Tests

GLI gave us the files and Rake tasks we need to start running unit tests, but let's go over the basics so you can set up unit testing for any project. We'll need to do two things: configure our Rakefile to run unit tests and create one or more files that contain our unit tests.

Setting it up in our Rakefile is simple, since rake includes the class Rake::TestTask, which sets up a rake task for running unit tests. We simply require the right module and set it up like so:

tolerate_gracefully/todo_unit_tests/Rakefile

```
require 'rake/testtask'
Rake::TestTask.new do |t|
  t.libs << "test"
  t.test_files = FileList['test/tc_*.rb']
end
```

We can now run unit tests in any file in the directory test that starts with the prefix tc_ by typing rake test.

Next, we need to create at least one file to run. All we have to do is create a file that contains a class that extends Test::Unit::TestCase and has at least one method that starts with the prefix test_. When we do this, rake test will run each test_ method as a unit test. Let's see it in action:

```
require 'test/unit'

class TaskTest < Test::Unit::TestCase
  def test_that_passes
    assert true
  end

  def test_that_fails
    assert false
  end
end
```

Now, we run our two tests and see what happens:

```
$ rake test
Started
F.
Finished in 0.003429 seconds.

  1) Failure:
test_that_fails(TaskTest)
    ./test/tc_task.rb:36:in `test_that_fails'
<false> is not true.

2 tests, 2 assertions, 1 failures, 0 errors
rake aborted!

(See full trace by running task with --trace)
```

One test passed, and the other failed. This gives us an idea of what to expect when writing and running unit tests. Let's remove these fake tests and write a real test for the code we just extracted.

Writing Unit Tests

Unlike our acceptance tests, our unit tests should not interact with the outside world; we want to test our code in complete isolation. This is the only way we can be sure that every aspect of the tests we write can be controlled. For our purposes here, it means we have to figure out how to prevent the call to File.open from opening an actual file on the filesystem.

What we'll do is *stub* the open call. Stubbing is a way to change the behavior of a method temporarily so that it behaves in a predictable way as part of a unit test. The open source library Mocha[3] allows us to do just that. When we include it in our tests, Mocha adds a stubs method to every single object in Ruby (including the class object File) that allows us to replace the default behavior of any method with new behavior.

To see this in action, let's test that add_task raises an exception when no tasks are passed in. Since File.open takes a block and we need that block to execute (that's where all the code in add_task is), we'll use the method yields, provided by Mocha, to stub open so that it simply executes the block it was given. We'll then pass in an empty array to new_task and use the method assert_raises, provided by Test::Unit, to assert that new_task raises an exception.

```
tolerate_gracefully/todo_unit_tests/test/tc_task.rb
include Todo

def test_raises_error_when_no_tasks
  File.stubs(:open).yields("")

  ex = assert_raises RuntimeError do
    new_task("foo.txt",[])
  end
  expected = "You must provide tasks on the command-line or standard input"
  assert_equal expected, ex.message
end
```

Notice how we also include the Todo module here so that our tests have access to the method we're testing. Back to the code, the first line of our test method does the stubbing. This tells File that when someone calls open to yield the empty string to the block given to open, instead of doing what open normally does. In effect, the variable todo_file in new_task will be set to the empty string instead of a File. This isn't a problem, since the path through the code we're simulating won't call any methods on it. Instead, new_task will realize that no tasks were added and raise an exception.

---

3.   http://mocha.rubyforge.org/

assert_raises verifies that the code inside the block given to it raises a RuntimeError. It also returns the instance of the exception that was thrown. We then make sure that the message of that exception matches the message we expect.

Since we've replaced open with our stub during the test, we also need to restore it back to normal once our test has run. Test::Unit will run the method teardown in our test class after each run (even if the test itself fails), so we can put this code there, using Mocha's unstub method to remove any stubs we've created.

tolerate_gracefully/todo_unit_tests/test/tc_task.rb

```ruby
def teardown
  File.unstub(:open)
end
```

Now we can run our test and see what happens:

```
$ rake test
Started
.
Finished in 0.000577 seconds.

1 tests, 2 assertions, 0 failures, 0 errors
```

Everything passed! Now that we know how to fake out File.open, we can write a complete set of tests for our new_task method. There are two major cases we need to cover: the normal execution of adding a new task and the case where we don't have permissions to read the file.

To test the normal case, we need to verify that the tasks we pass to new_task are written to the file. Since we don't want to actually write to the file, we'll use our newfound ability to stub the File.open method to capture what new_task writes out. We'll do this by yielding an instance of StringIO to the block given to File.open. StringIO looks and acts just like a real file, but it saves its data internally and not on the filesystem. We can pull that data out and examine it. That's exactly what we need to do, so let's see the test:

tolerate_gracefully/todo_unit_tests/test/tc_task.rb

```ruby
def test_proper_working
  string_io = StringIO.new
  File.stubs(:open).yields(string_io)

  new_task("foo.txt",["This is a task"])

  assert_match /^This is a task,/,string_io.string
end
```

When we call add_task now, the file that gets yielded will be our variable string_io. When add_task calls puts on it, it saves the string internally, which we can then examine via the string method on string_io. We assert that that string matches a regular expression containing our task name (we use a regexp here because the current date/time will also be written out).

Let's run this test and see what happens:

```
$ rake test
Started
..
Finished in 0.001007 seconds.

2 tests, 3 assertions, 0 failures, 0 errors
```

This test also passed. To prove that File.open did not create a file, we'll see if foo.txt is in our current directory:

```
$ ls foo.txt
ls: foo.txt: No such file or directory
```

The last case is the trickiest one and is the reason we've started writing unit tests; we want to make sure add_task gives a reasonable error message when the task list file cannot be written to. If this were to happen in real life, File.open would throw an Errno::EPERM exception. This exception gets its name from the C standard library's constant for a lack of permissions. We'll stub File.open to throw that error. We don't want add_task to throw that exception, however. We want it to throw a RuntimeError, and we want that exception to have a useful message that includes the message from the underlying exception. Let's see the test:

tolerate_gracefully/todo_unit_tests/test/tc_task.rb
```
def test_cannot_open_file
  ex_msg = "Operation not permitted"
  File.stubs(:open).raises(Errno::EPERM.new(ex_msg))
  ex = assert_raises RuntimeError do
    new_task("foo.txt",["This is a task"])
  end
  assert_match /^Couldn't open foo.txt for appending: #{ex_msg}/,ex.message
end
```

Now, when we run our unit test, it fails:

```
$ rake test
Started
F..
Finished in 0.008249 seconds.

  1) Failure:
test_error(TaskTest)
  [./test/tc_task.rb:44:in `test_error'
  mocha/integration/test_unit/ruby_version_186_and_above.rb:22:in `__send__'
```

```
    mocha/integration/test_unit/ruby_version_186_and_above.rb:22:in `run']:
<RuntimeError> exception expected but was
Class: <Errno::EPERM>
Message: <"Operation not permitted">
---Backtrace---
lib/mocha/exception_raiser.rb:12:in `evaluate'
lib/mocha/return_values.rb:20:in `next'
lib/mocha/expectation.rb:472:in `invoke'
lib/mocha/mock.rb:157:in `method_missing'
lib/mocha/class_method.rb:46:in `open'
./lib/todo/task.rb:4:in `new_task'
./test/tc_task.rb:45:in `test_error'
./test/tc_task.rb:44:in `test_error'
mocha/integration/test_unit/ruby_version_186_and_above.rb:22:in `__send__'
mocha/integration/test_unit/ruby_version_186_and_above.rb:22:in `run'
---------------

3 tests, 4 assertions, 1 failures, 0 errors
rake aborted!
```

We get a big, nasty backtrace, and we see that instead of getting a RuntimeError, we got an Errno::EPERM. This isn't surprising, since our test forced that to happen. What's missing here is the code to translate that exception into a RuntimeError. We'll fix it by catching SystemCallError (which is the superclass of all Errno::-style errors) and throwing a RuntimeError with a more helpful message.

tolerate_gracefully/todo_unit_tests/lib/todo/todo.rb
```ruby
def new_task(filename,task_names)
  File.open(filename,'a+') do |todo_file|
    tasks = 0
    task_names.each do |task|
      todo_file.puts [task,Time.now].join(',')
      tasks += 1
    end
    if tasks == 0
      raise "You must provide tasks on the command-line or standard input"
    end
  end
➤ rescue SystemCallError => ex
➤   raise RuntimeError,"Couldn't open #{filename} for appending: #{ex.message}"
end
```

Now, our test passes with flying colors:

```
$ rake test
Started
...
Finished in 0.00192 seconds.

3 tests, 5 assertions, 0 failures, 0 errors
```

We've covered all the paths through this method. To continue testing todo with unit tests, we'll continue extracting code into testable units and writing tests. The ability to stub out methods is very powerful and enables us to get very good test coverage. This is one of the benefits of working with a dynamic language like Ruby.

8.3 A Word About Test-Driven Development

We've built our apps a bit backward from the accepted practice in the Ruby community. You *should* be writing your tests first, using them to drive the development of features. We didn't do that; we started with code and added tests afterward. This was done purely to make it easier to learn concepts about command-line app development. We needed to know *what* to test before learning *how* to test. To be clear, we are *not* endorsing "test-last development."

To write command-line apps using Test-Driven Development (TDD), you can apply the same principles we've learned here, but just start with the tests instead of the code. (See *Kent Beck's Book on TDD* [Bec02].) The simplest thing to do is to start using Cucumber and Aruba to identify the user interface and user-facing features of your app. Write one scenario at a time, get that working, and move on to a new scenario. Repeat this process until you have the basic "happy paths" through your app working. Simulate a few error cases if you can, but at that point, you'll want to turn your attention to unit tests, extracting your mostly working code into testable units and putting them through the ringer to iron out all the edge cases.

8.4 Moving On

We only scratched the surface of the art of software testing, but we went through a whirlwind tour of everything you'll need to get started for testing command-line apps. We saw some real challenges with testing our apps, as well as several techniques to deal with them. By manipulating the environment, setting up test-specific infrastructure, and mocking system calls, we can simulate almost anything that might happen when our app runs.

Toward the end, when we learned about unit testing, we talked briefly about refactoring. Refactoring is difficult without tests, but with a good suite of tests, we can safely change the internal design of our code. We got a taste of that when we extracted our business logic out of bin/todo and put it into lib/todo/task.rb so we could unit test it. In the next chapter, we'll learn some patterns and techniques for organizing our code so that it's easy to maintain, test, and enhance.

Be Easy to Maintain

We know how to make an easy-to-use, helpful app that interacts with the system as easily as its users yet is highly flexible. In the previous chapter, we learned how to test such an app. We're almost done with our journey through command-line app development. What we haven't talked about is how to manage our apps in the face of increasing complexity. We imagined a version of our todo app that integrated with JIRA, a commercial issue-tracking system. What if we decided to open source that app and users wanted it to integrate with other issue-tracking systems? How do we make sure we can contain the complexity of a growing, popular app?

You've already learned the first step in writing a maintainable application: a good test suite. With a solid set of tests, we can be free to make changes to *how* our app works. These sorts of changes aren't for the users (at least not directly); they're for us. Reorganizing our code makes it easier for us to work with it, as well as for others to understand it so they can help us. This chapter deals with this problem in two parts. In the first, we'll talk about where files should go and how they should generally be structured (we got a taste of this in the previous chapter when we extracted code to write unit tests). The second part will demonstrate a few techniques for reorganizing code by applying some simple *design patterns* to our running example apps. Ideally, seeing some refactoring in action will give you the confidence you need to do the same with your own apps.

9.1 Dividing Code into Multiple Files

In the previous chapter, in order to test the main logic of our task-management app todo, we created the file lib/todo/task.rb, created a class Task that was inside the module Todo, and put some logic into the add_task method. We glossed over the reasons for this, but what we did was a standard way of organizing code in Ruby. This section will explain the how and why of code organization.

You might wonder why we should even bother storing our code in multiple files; it does add a certain amount of complexity to our application because code is no longer in one place. Keeping the code all in our executable carries complexity as well. In the previous chapter, we saw that we couldn't unit test code that was stored in there; if we were to require an executable into a test, the executable would run before we got a chance to set up our test. There is another reason, as well.

Keeping our code organized across several files will make it *easier* to find things once our app gets to a certain level of complexity. Understanding an app that is made up of a single 1,000+ line file can be hard. Even todo, which consists of about 120 lines of code, is already showing some problems. The vast majority of the file sets up the user interface. The actual logic of what our app does is buried several layers deep and spread throughout the file. If we wanted to get an understanding of what a task *is* and how the code manages the task list, we'd have to bounce all over the file to figure it out.

So, by organizing code in several files, we can make things much clearer. We'll look in one file to understand the user interface, another for the logic of task management, another for writing output for the user, and so on. All it takes is following a few conventions. First we'll talk about the mechanics of accessing files outside of our executable, and then we'll learn some conventions for organizing code within those "outside" files.

Configuring Code to Find External Files

In Ruby, it's customary to place most of your code in files in (or in a subdirectory of) the lib directory. (Some Rubyists prefer to put *all* code here.) We'll keep user interface code in our executable but place all non-UI-specific code in files in lib. We'll talk about how to organize the code inside there in a moment. The main issue you can run into when moving your code out of the main executable is being able to find it so it can be required at runtime. When you use require, Ruby searches the *load path* for that file. By default, the load path won't include your application's lib directory. Since we're deploying with RubyGems (see Chapter 7, *Distribute Painlessly*, on page 101), this problem is easily solved in the gemspec.

As you may recall, the gemspec includes the list of files to package with your application. The gemspec also includes an array of *require paths*, which are all the paths, relative to your project root, that should be added to the load path when your application starts. Setting this is straightforward:

be_easy_to_maintain/todo/todo.gemspec

```
  s.files = %w(
bin/todo
lib/todo_version.rb
  )
➤  s.require_paths << 'lib'
```

When gem installs your RubyGem, it will make sure that the executable it puts in the installing user's path will set up the Ruby environment so that your files in lib can be found. It also means that this line from bin/todo that sets up the load path is unnecessary. (However, this is *not* the case when using a non-RubyGems installation method. Further, removing this line will have some slight implications for running our app locally and for running our tests. See *Developing Locally Without Modifying the Load Path*, on page 144.)

be_easy_to_maintain/todo/bin/todo

```
# This line can be removed
#$LOAD_PATH << File.expand_path(File.dirname(__FILE__) + '/../lib')

require 'rubygems'
require 'gli'
require 'todo_version'
require 'todo/task'
```

Once we have our code in the lib directory and our gemspec is updated to add it to the load path, there's now a question of where code goes in files.

Organizing Code Within Files

Now that we can access code from files in lib, we need to know the best way to organize those files. There are three conventions to follow:

- Each class should be namespaced inside a module named for the project.

- Each class should be in its own file, with the filename and path based on the class's name and namespace.

- A single file inside lib, named for the project, should require all other files in lib.

There might be a few unfamiliar terms in there, but don't worry, it'll be clear in a moment. Let's look at our first convention, which tells us how to name files based on the code they contain.

Developing Locally Without Modifying the Load Path

Since RubyGems takes care of setting up our app's load path at runtime, it's considered bad practice to modify the load path (using the variable $LOAD_PATH) in application code. Avoiding this bad practice causes us a problem, however.

```
$ bin/todo help
custom_require.rb:36:in `gem_original_require': no such file to load --
  todo_version (LoadError)
    from custom_require.rb:36:in `require'
    from bin/todo:8
```

When run locally, our app cannot find the files in lib. If we were to run our Cucumber features, we would have the same problem. The fix for both is the environment variable RUBYLIB. RUBYLIB is a delimited list of paths that are added to the load path. The delimiter is platform-specific (colon on UNIX and semicolon on Windows), so fixing it for Cucumber is a bit trickier than in our shell. We don't want to require users to set it in their environment, so we apply the same technique we did when dealing with the user's home directory; we modify RUBYLIB inside ENV.

```
be_easy_to_maintain/todo/features/support/env.rb
LIB_DIR = File.join(File.expand_path(File.dirname(__FILE__)),'..','..','lib')

Before do
  @original_rubylib = ENV['RUBYLIB']
  ENV['RUBYLIB'] = LIB_DIR + File::PATH_SEPARATOR + ENV['RUBYLIB'].to_s
end

After do
  ENV['RUBYLIB'] = @original_rubylib
end
```

To run locally, we could do the same thing like so:

```
$ RUBYLIB=lib bin/todo help
usage: todo [global options] command [command options]

# etc.
```

An alterantive, since we're using Bundler, is to use bundle exec:

```
$ bundle exec bin/todo help
usage: todo [global options] command [command options]

# etc.
```

These two forms are slightly different; bundle exec will run our app with the *exact* versions of each gem as specified in our Gemfile.lock, which is likely what we want. It's also easier to type bundle exec than RUBYLIB=lib on the command line.

Namespacing Classes

In Ruby, classes can be namespaced using modules. You may recall that, when we extracted our code from todo into lib/todo/task.rb, we placed the class Task inside the module Todo. This *namespaced* Task inside Todo, making the class's complete name Todo::Task. Since Ruby has open classes, if someone else had a class named Task and we *didn't* namespace our Task class, we'd be adding methods to the existing Task class, and things would likely not work properly.

To avoid this situation, all of your classes should be namespaced, and the module in which to place them should be named for your app, in our case Todo. Note that you should "camelize" the module name, so for our db_backup MySQL backup app, its module would be DbBackup.

Naming Files According to Their Full Classname

Once a class is in a namespace, the path/name to the file containing that class's source code should match the namespace. In our case, the class Todo::Task is stored in a file named todo/task.rb (relative to lib). If we created a new class named Todo::TicketSystem, its source would be stored in todo/ticket_system.rb (note how we use the underscore version of the classname). If we had a class named Todo::TicketSystem::JIRA, this would be stored in todo/ticket_system/jira.rb (again, relative to lib).

This leads to a proliferation of files, and it might seem that our executable is going to have a lot of require statements at the top. Further, it seems that every time we add a new file, the executable has to change to include it. We can avoid this by using the third convention: having one file dedicated to requireing the correct files.

Requiring All Files from a Single File in lib

We'd like to write the following in the executable and get every file and class we needed:

```
require 'todo'
```

We can make this happen by including all of our require statements in lib/todo.rb:

```
require 'todo/task'
require 'todo/ticket_system'
require 'todo/ticket_system/jira'
```

We *will* have to maintain this file as we add new classes, but it does keep our executable clean, and our Cucumber features will instantly fail if we forget to update this file.

We've now learned the mechanics of organizing bits of code into external files and making sure our application can find them at runtime. In Ruby, those "bits" are classes and modules, and making sure that the right code goes into the right class or module is just as important as where our files are located. In the next section, we'll briefly discuss why, and then we'll see some examples of how to design the internals of an application using classes and modules effectively.

9.2 Designing Code for Maintainability

Everything we've learned so far about making our codebase maintainable has been encapsulated with clear and simple guidelines. The conventions we've just discussed are shared by Rubyists everywhere and will make it very easy for anyone, including you, to navigate your code. This means that bugs get fixed faster, and new features can be pushed out quickly, which means users win, the app's developers win, and you win.

However, there's more to maintainability than just an organized file structure. The internal design of our application is just as important. Since Ruby is an object-oriented language, the *internal design* of a Ruby application revolves around organizing code into classes and modules. Achieving good object-oriented design is well outside the scope of this book, but suffice it to say, the more sense the code makes, the easier it is to enhance, fix, and work with. Let's look at the code for our task management app, todo.

```
be_easy_to_maintain/todo/bin/todo
file.readlines.each do |todo|
  name,created,completed = todo.chomp.split(/,/)
  if options[:format] == 'pretty'
    # Use the pretty-print format
    printf("%2d - %s\n",index,name)
    printf("      %-10s %s\n","Created:",created)
    printf("      %-10s %s\n","Completed:",completed) if completed
  elsif options[:format] == 'csv'
    # Use the machine-readable CSV format
    complete_flag = completed ? "C" : "U"
    printf("%d,%s,%s,%s,%s\n",index,name,complete_flag,created,completed)
  end
  index += 1
end
```

This code is doing a lot of things at once: it's parsing the tasks from the external tasklist file, it's formatting them (based on the user's selection), and it's iterating over all the tasks. Suppose we wanted to add a new command-line switch to allow the user to hide completed tasks. We'd have to add even more code to this block. Understanding this seemingly simple bit of code requires keeping our brains focused on many levels of the software: the user interface, the domain of "task management," and the internals of how we store our tasks. Classes are just the thing to sort this out.

There are many, many books on object-oriented design, and there are many design patterns that help solve common problems (see *The Gang of Four* [GHJV95] book for an overview of several common patterns). What we'll do here is apply some of those patterns to the problems in our code. This will demonstrate how to apply these patterns, but it will also help give you a bit of direction when you decide that your code's internal structure needs a cleanup.

We'll start by encapsulating everything about tasks in our app by expanding our Task. Then, we'll apply a pattern called Factory Method to allow us to easily construct our tasks from the task list file's contents. Finally, we'll abstract all of that formatting code by using the Strategy pattern. This way, the code inside list's action block will be cleaner and easier to understand.

Encapsulating Data and Code into Classes

The remainder of this chapter depends on our data being stored in an object, not as "loose" variables. Right now, we have name, created, and completed in our code to represent a particular task, as well as its current state. If we can encapsulate these attributes inside our Task class, it will simplify things quite a bit. This change sets the stage for further changes, so its positive effect won't be seen until the end of this section.

We already have a Task class from our previous refactoring from Chapter 8, *Test, Test, Test*, on page 117. That class has only one method, and we created it to have a "unit" to test. Let's expand this class by adding the attributes of a task to it.

be_easy_to_maintain/todo/lib/todo/task.rb
```
attr_reader :name,
            :created_date,
            :completed_date

def initialize(name,created_date,completed_date)
  @name = name
  @created_date = created_date
```

```
    @completed_date = completed_date
end

def completed?
  !completed_date.nil?
end
```

Now we have a single source of information about any task in our system. A task is formally defined as a name, a date of creation, and a date of completion. It also has a notion of being completed or not (the completed? method). This, in and of itself, will actually increase the size of our code as currently designed. As we said, this is setting the stage. The usefulness of this class will become apparent by the end of the section.

Using the Factory Method Pattern to Control How Objects Are Created

Currently, the way in which tasks are written to and read from the tasklist file is spread out across the executable. If we centralize how this is done, we can simplify our main code and provide another testable unit to ensure the quality of our application. We'll add a class method to Task that, given a file-name, reads it and returns a list of Task instances. Since this method creates new objects, it's called a *factory method*. Here's what it looks like:

be_easy_to_maintain/todo/lib/todo/task.rb
```
class Task
  def self.from_file(file)
    tasks = []
    file.readlines.each do |line|
      name,created,completed = line.chomp.split(/,/)
      tasks << Task.new(name,created,completed)
    end
    tasks
  end
end
```

With our factory method from_file vending instances of Task, our list command code is vastly simplified:

be_easy_to_maintain/todo/bin/todo
```
Todo::Task.from_file(tasklist).each do |task|

  # ... formatting code

end
```

Notice how the code just *reads* better. Say it out loud: "tasks equal tasks from the file task list." More importantly, we've now encapsulated the individual bits of a task inside the Task class, and the details of parsing the file are a class method of Task. If we were to add another attribute to a task—say, a priority—our code inside the list command won't have to change. We're keeping the general outline of the list command's algorithm separate from the details of how the tasks are stored in the task list file.

Of course, we still have all that code to deal with for formatting a task for output. Let's simplify that next.

Organizing Multiple Ways of Doing Something with the Strategy Pattern

Other than mixing in low-level details to our high-level list command code, there's another situation that will make this code even harder to maintain. Let's assume JSON as a choice for formatting output. To accommodate that, we'll have to update our documentation string, add another elsif block, and implement the format.

Whenever we have many ways of doing conceptually the same thing, the *Strategy pattern* can usually simplify the code. This pattern involves placing the code for each way of doing something (i.e., each strategy) in a different class, each of which has the same interface. We then locate the correct class at runtime and apply the strategy. Instead of seeing the actual strategy classes first, let's look at the complete picture that we're aiming for:

```
be_easy_to_maintain/todo/bin/todo
command :list do |c|
  output_formats = {
    'csv' => Todo::Format::CSV.new,
    'pretty' => Todo::Format::Pretty.new,
  }
  c.desc 'Format of the output (pretty for TTY, csv otherwise)'
  c.arg_name output_formats.keys.join('|')
  c.flag :format
  c.action do |global_options,options,args|
    formatter = output_formats[options[:format]]
    File.open(global_options[:filename]) do |tasklist|
      index = 1
      Todo::Task.from_file(tasklist).each do |task|
        formatter.format(index,task)
        index += 1
      end
    end
  end
end
```

The Hash named output_formats is a map of formatting strategies. The keys are the names the user will specify on the command line; we join them with pipes to generate the documentation string for arg_name. We then use the value of the --format flag to locate the correct strategy class. We assume that all strategy classes have a method format that takes the current index as well as the task to format.

Now, our list code is very clear and clean; we see that we're reading the tasks from a file and then formatting each one for the user. Adding a new format is as simple as adding an entry to our output_formats hash; that's it!

```ruby
output_formats = {
  'csv' => Todo::Format::CSV.new,
  'pretty' => Todo::Format::Pretty.new,
➤ 'json' => Todo::Format::JSON.new,
}
```

Seeing the end state, it's easy to think about how to implement our formatting strategies. Here's how they ended up:

be_easy_to_maintain/todo/lib/todo/format/csv.rb
```ruby
module Todo
  module Format
    class CSV
      def format(index,task)
        complete_flag = task.completed? ? "C" : "U"
        printf("%d,%s,%s,%s,%s\n",
                index,
                task.name,
                complete_flag,
                task.created_date,
                task.completed_date)
      end
    end
  end
end
```

be_easy_to_maintain/todo/lib/todo/format/pretty.rb
```ruby
module Todo
  module Format
    class Pretty
      def format(index,task)
        printf("%2d - %s\n",index,task.name)
        printf("    %-10s %s\n","Created:",task.created_date)
        if task.completed?
          printf("    %-10s %s\n","Completed:",task.completed_date)
        end
      end
    end
  end
end
```

With our code redesigned to take advantage of some common design patterns, we've made the following programming tasks easier to do:

- Add new output formats
- Add new attributes of a task
- Isolate and fix bugs by unit testing
- Parse or format tasks in other parts of the codebase

All this adds up to fixing bugs and adding new features much more easily. In addition, since these patterns are well-known among developers, others will be able to more easily help you keep your apps working and up-to-date. These aren't the only patterns that exist; there are countless ways of organizing your code to make it easier to work with. Ideally, this has given you some ideas about how to structure your code for maximum ease of development.

9.3 Moving On

We've learned two things in this chapter, both to help make our code easier to navigate, easier to understand, easier to enhance, and easier to work with. By putting code into the right place in our project, we can keep things organized and comprehensible. By applying design patterns to the structure of our code, we make it clear to ourselves and other developers how the application works. We've set ourselves up to quickly fix bugs and easily add new features.

You're in the home stretch now and have learned everything you need to make awesome command-line applications. You've learned all the rules, so now it's time to break some of them. Thus far, we've stuck to the "UNIX Way" of machine-parseable output and no interactive input. What if we want to do something fancier? We saw how Cucumber uses color to assist its users. You've likely used (and appreciated) a SQL client that formats its output in tabular form, as well as takes interactive input. How can we use these techniques in our apps? More importantly, *should* we?

In the next chapter, we'll see how to add color, formatting, and interactive input to our apps, making them potentially more useful and even more fun! Of course, we'll also learn when we should and when we *should not* apply these techniques.

Add Color, Formatting, and Interactivity

We could end this book right here, and you'd be fully capable of making awesome command-line applications. The conventions, techniques, and rules we've discussed are always safe to use and will never steer you wrong. But, this is not the end of what we can learn. If you followed along during Chapter 8, *Test, Test, Test,* on page 117, you saw that Cucumber produced colorful output. If you've ever used a SQL client, you've seen that it both formats output in tables *and* provides an interactive prompt, complete with history and tab completion.

In general, your apps should not provide any of these things; avoiding color, formatted output, and user interaction make our apps interoperable with other systems and apps. Sometimes, however, these features are either called for or can greatly enhance the experience of your users. Imagine a SQL client that didn't format output in tables; it would be very difficult to use for examining a database.

This chapter is about the when and how of creating a "rich" user interface. We'll discuss three ways to create such an enhanced user interface. First, we'll look at using color, specifically how to use ANSI escape sequences via the open source gem rainbow. Next, we'll learn about formatted output, using the open source library terminal-table to create tabular output. Finally, we'll talk about creating an interactive user experience using readline, which is built in to Ruby. We'll talk about *when* to consider using each feature before diving in and seeing how it works.

One rule applies to all of these situations, and it's a rule you should *never* break. No matter how much you enhance the output formatting or how much of an interactive experience you want to make, *always provide a UNIX-style, noninteractive, machine-friendly mode.* We saw how to do this in Chapter 4, *Play Well with Others,* on page 53, and starting from a machine-friendly interface is always a good first step. You may choose to default to colorful output or interactive input, but *always* allow the user to use the app in a vanilla UNIX-compliant way through the use of command-line options.

With that being said, let's see how to add color to our apps.

10.1 Adding Color Using ANSI Escape Sequences

Cucumber is a great example of a command-line app that uses color effectively. Cucumber wants to motivate the user to work in a certain way. The user first writes a feature file and runs it, seeing a stream of red steps output to the terminal. As the user works to "fix" each step, the steps turn green until all the steps of all scenarios of the feature are passing, showing a pleasant stream of green steps to the terminal. Working this way can be quite satisfying, and Cucumber's use of color is a huge part of this.

We'll learn how to make our apps use color, by using the rainbow gem, which provides an easy way to manipulate the ANSI escape sequences that allow a terminal to show color. Before that, however, we must understand when it's OK, and our observation of Cucumber provides a good example.

When to Use Color

The authors of Cucumber have a strong opinion about how to use it, and their use of color reflects this opinion. You might think of this as some form of negative, and then positive, reinforcement, but it's really just reporting information to the user in a way that can be scanned and quickly understood. If you see a lot of green, you don't need to read further: everything is OK. If you see some red or yellow fly by, you'll need to scroll back to see what the problem was.

If your app has a feature that reports some sort of status, especially among a large set of data, color could be a great benefit to your users. Suppose you have an application that monitors processes; you might show the process name in green if it's functioning properly, yellow if it's responding slowly, and red if it's not responding at all. A user running your program can quickly get a summary of what's going on without having to read each line carefully.

Even if your app isn't strictly monitoring things, color is still a great way to catch the user's eye. Suppose your app generates a lot of terminal output; coloring error messages red will help alert the user that something is wrong. Without the colored output, the user will have to look much more closely to see error messages scroll by. Or consider ack,[1] which is an alternative to grep. It uses color and styling to draw the user's attention to parts of a line that matched the search string.

You could also use color purely for decoration. The OS X package manager homebrew[2] uses colorized output for no functional reason but essentially to "look pretty." This may seem like a silly reason to use color, and you certainly shouldn't just add color for the sake of color, but you also shouldn't discount aesthetics. This is much more subjective, but if you think color really will enhance the user experience, by all means, go for it!

A slight word of warning, however. A surprisingly high number of people in the world are color-blind,[3] almost 9 percent, and cannot easily distinguish certain colors. As such, your app should *never* rely on color alone to be useful. Use color only to enhance information that's being presented, never as information itself.

How to Use Color

Colored output on the command line is accomplished via the use of ANSI escape sequences.[4] These sequences of bytes are nonprintable characters that most terminal emulators will interpret as changes to styling and color. Generating them by hand is cumbersome and results in difficult-to-understand strings of text. Fortunately, there is a plethora of Ruby libraries to generate them for us. We're going to use rainbow,[5] which provides a readable, low-impact API as well as a few other handy features that we'll see (another popular library is term-ansicolor[6]).

To see how to use rainbow to add color and styling to our output, we're going to enhance todo's "pretty" format to help the user better understand their task list. If you're reading this in a black-and-white format, you might want to follow along on your computer so you can see the effects of the changes we're making.

First let's review the current "pretty" format of todo by adding a few tasks, completing one, and getting the list. (Recall that we must use bundle exec since we are running out of our source tree for this example; users of todo will, of

---

1. http://betterthangrep.com/
2. http://mxcl.github.com/homebrew
3. http://en.wikipedia.org/wiki/Color_blindness
4. http://en.wikipedia.org/wiki/ANSI_escape_code
5. http://github.com/sickill/rainbow
6. http://flori.github.com/term-ansicolor/

course, be able to run todo on its own, as discussed in Chapter 9, *Be Easy to Maintain*, on page 141.)

```
$ bundle exec bin/todo new
Reading new tasks from stdin...
Design database schema
Get access to production logs
Code Review
Implement model objects for new scheme
^D
$ bundle exec bin/todo done 3
$ bundle exec bin/todo list
1 - Design database schema
    Created:    Sun Oct 30 12:53:11 -0400 2011
2 - Get access to production logs
    Created:    Sun Oct 30 12:53:11 -0400 2011
3 - Code Review
    Created:    Sun Oct 30 12:53:11 -0400 2011
    Completed: Sun Oct 30 13:00:05 -0400 2011
4 - Implement model objects for new schema
    Created:    Sun Oct 30 12:53:11 -0400 2011
```

Let's enhance the output of list as follows:

- Show the task name in a brighter/bolder font (the ANSI escape sequences provide two version of each color: a normal color and a brighter/bolder version). This will make it easier for the user to use the most important information in the task list.

- Show completed tasks in green. This will give the user a sense of satisfaction; the more green the user sees, the more they've accomplished.

Both of these formatting options are available via ANSI escape sequences and therefore are available via rainbow. rainbow works by adding a few new methods to Ruby's built-in String class. The methods we'll use are color and bright, which will set the color of and brighten the string on which they are called, respectively. Since we've extracted all the code for the pretty formatter to the class Todo::Format::Pretty, we know exactly where to go to add this feature. But first we need to add rainbow to our gemspec:

break_rules/todo/todo.gemspec
```
require File.join([File.dirname(__FILE__),'lib','todo_version.rb'])
spec = Gem::Specification.new do |s|
  s.name = 'todo'
  s.version = '0.0.1'

  # ...

  s.add_dependency('gli')
```

```
➤     s.add_dependency('rainbow')
    end
```

We then install it locally using Bundler:

```
$ bundle install
bundle install
Fetching source index for http://rubygems.org/
Using gherkin (2.4.21)
Using cucumber (1.0.6)
Using aruba (0.4.6)
➤ Installing rainbow (1.1.1)
Using gli (1.3.5)
```

Windows users should also install the gem win32console, which adapts the Windows command prompt to ASCII escape sequences.

Adding colored output is going to make our formatter a bit more complex, so let's take things one step at a time. First we'll use bright to call out the task name:

```
break_rules/todo/lib/todo/format/pretty.rb
require 'rainbow'

module Todo
  module Format
    class Pretty
      def format(index,task)
➤       printf("%2d - %s\n",index,task.name.bright)
        printf("    %-10s %s\n","Created:",task.created_date)
        if task.completed?
          printf("      %-10s %s\n","Completed:",task.completed_date)
        end
      end
    end
  end
end
```

When we run list, we can now see that the task names are bolder, as in Figure 6, *Using bright results in task names that stand out*, on page 158.

Next, we'll color the entire string green when the task is completed. This will require some restructuring, since we are currently using printf to output directly to the standard output. Instead, we'll use sprintf, which simply returns the string, which we can then optionally apply color to, before outputting it to the standard output.

To handle the case where we *don't* want to color the output, we'll use a special color provided by rainbow named :default. This color just means "do not apply special colors." We can use this as the argument to color, unless the task is

```
>bundle exec bin/todo.rb list
 1 - Design database schema
      Created:   Sun Oct 30 12:53:11 -0400 2011
 2 - Get access to production logs
      Created:   Sun Oct 30 12:53:11 -0400 2011
 3 - Code Review
      Created:   Sun Oct 30 12:53:11 -0400 2011
      Completed: Sun Oct 30 13:00:05 -0400 2011
 4 - Implement model objects for new schema
      Created:   Sun Oct 30 12:53:11 -0400 2011
>
```

Figure 6—Using bright results in task names that stand out.

completed, and then we'll use :green. We have to change every line, so read this code a few times to make sure you see the differences:

break_rules/todo/lib/todo/format/pretty.rb
```
def format(index,task)
  color = :default
  if task.completed?
    color = :green
  end

  puts sprintf("%2d - %s",index,task.name.bright).color(color)
  puts sprintf("     %-10s %s","Created:",task.created_date).color(color)
  if task.completed?
    puts sprintf("     %-10s %s","Completed:",task.completed_date).color(color)
  end
end
```

Now our completed task pops out as shown in Figure 7, *Completed tasks show in green*, on page 159.

As you can see, formatting "stacks": the task name of our completed task is both bright *and* green. This is how the ANSI escape sequences work, and it gives us great power over the formatting of our output. Before we move on, let's cover a handy feature of rainbow that you'll find useful when providing a noncolored version of your output.

Suppose a user's terminal colors are set in such a way that our chosen colors make it difficult to read the output. We want the user to be able to use the "pretty" format but without the colors. Rainbow provides an attribute enabled that will globally disable colors. This turns all of rainbow's methods into no-ops, meaning we don't need to special case our code or create another formatter. We'll handle this entirely in our executable:

```
>bundle exec bin/todo.rb list
 1 - Design database schema
       Created:   Sun Oct 30 12:53:11 -0400 2011
 2 - Get access to production logs
       Created:   Sun Oct 30 12:53:11 -0400 2011
 3 - Code Review
       Created:   Sun Oct 30 12:53:11 -0400 2011
       Completed: Sun Oct 30 13:00:05 -0400 2011
 4 - Implement model objects for new schema
       Created:   Sun Oct 30 12:53:11 -0400 2011
>
```

Figure 7—Completed tasks show in green.

break_rules/todo/bin/todo
```
command :list do |c|

    # ...

➤   c.desc "Don't use colors"
➤   c.switch 'no-color'

    c.action do |global_options,options,args|
➤     if options[:'no-color']
➤       Sickill::Rainbow.enabled = false
➤     end

      # ...

    end
end
```

When we run todo list with the --no-color option, we no longer see any colors or formatting, as shown in Figure 8, *Colors are disabled*, on page 160.

Colors aren't the only way to make our output easier to understand by the user. Formatting using tables can be an effective way to present certain types of data, as we'll see in the next section.

10.2 Formatting Output with Tables

In Chapter 4, *Play Well with Others*, on page 53, we discussed using CSV format to organize output, where each line would represent a record and each comma-separated value would represent a field. We even updated todo to use this format to make it easier to integrate with other programs. Humans have a hard time reading CSV-formatted data, instead finding it easier to view such

```
○ ○ ○                        todo — bash — 50×15
>bundle exec bin/todo.rb list --no-color
 1 - Design database schema
     Created:   Sun Oct 30 12:53:11 -0400 2011
 2 - Get access to production logs
     Created:   Sun Oct 30 12:53:11 -0400 2011
 3 - Code Review
     Created:   Sun Oct 30 12:53:11 -0400 2011
     Completed: Sun Oct 30 13:00:05 -0400 2011
 4 - Implement model objects for new schema
     Created:   Sun Oct 30 12:53:11 -0400 2011
>
```

Figure 8—Colors are disabled.

data in a tabular format. This is why spreadsheet programs like Microsoft Excel can import CSV files and display their data in tables. It's also why most SQL database clients show their output in tables; it's a great way to look at a lot of data in an organized fashion.

Using the gem terminal-table, it's very easy to produce tabular output from our command-line app, but first it's good to understand when it's appropriate to do so.

When to Format Output as Tables

You'll want to use a tabular view for apps that allow the user to examine large amounts of "records and fields" data. The content of a database is a good example. You should, of course, always provide a machine-readable format, but a tabular view can be handy for users who might want to examine some data before piping it to another program.

How to Format Output As Tables

To see how to format output as tables using terminal-tables, let's add a new formatter to todo that will output the tasks in a tabular format. We want the output to look something like this:

```
$ bundle exec todo/bin/todo --format=table
+----+--------------------------------------+------------+------------+
| id | name                                 | created    | completed  |
+----+--------------------------------------+------------+------------+
|  1 | Design database schema               | 2011-10-03 |            |
|  2 | Get access to production logs        | 2011-09-27 |            |
|  3 | Code Review                          | 2011-10-29 | 2011-10-30 |
|  4 | Implement model objects for new schema | 2011-10-13 |          |
+----+--------------------------------------+------------+------------+
```

Notice how the cell size is just big enough to hold the largest piece of data, including the header. Notice further that the numbers in the ID column are right-aligned. We'll see that this is very easy to accomplish. Because of the refactoring of our code from Chapter 9, *Be Easy to Maintain*, on page 141, it will be easy to create a new formatter, although we'll first need to make a slight change to the way the output is done.

terminal table works by creating an instance of Terminal::Table. You then use the << method to append rows to the table, followed by a call to to_s to generate the output. Since our formatter classes currently have no way of knowing when output starts or completes, there's no obvious place to put the setup code or the call to to_s that we need to make the formatting work.

So, we'll add two new methods to the formatter interface. (The *interface* of a set of classes is the set of methods that they all implement; right now our formatter classes' interface is just the format method.) We'll add a method before that is called before any tasks are given to format and a method after that will be called after all the tasks have been given to format.

Before we begin, we'll need to make sure that the gem terminal-table is in our gemspec as a dependency and that we run bundle install to install it locally (we'll omit the code, since you should be well familiar with this by now). Once that's done, we'll use terminal-table to implement our new formatter, called Todo::Format::Table, which will live in lib/todo/format/table.rb, as per our conventions in Chapter 9, *Be Easy to Maintain*, on page 141.

break_rules/todo_tables/lib/todo/format/table.rb

```ruby
require 'terminal-table'

module Todo
  module Format
    class Table
      def before
        @@table = Terminal::Table.new :headings => %w(id name created completed)
        @@table.align_column(0,:right)
      end

      def format(index,task)
        row = []
        row << index
        row << task.name
        row << as_date(task.created_date)
        if task.completed?
          row << as_date(task.completed_date)
        else
          row << ''
        end
```

① ② ③

```
        @@table << row
      end

      def after
④       puts @@table.to_s
      end

      private

⑤     def as_date(string)
        Time.parse(string).strftime("%Y-%m-%d")
      end
    end
  end
end
```

This is a big block of code, so let's focus on a few of the important statements, which are called out in the listing with line numbers:

① Here we create our Terminal::Table instance. We specify the names of the headings as an array. If we omitted this option, the table would still work but wouldn't have any headings.

② Here is where we make sure that the ID field is right-aligned. The first field is 0 and the default alignment is :left, so we specify :right for the first field. We could also use :center to center the data in a cell.

③ Here we format the timestamps to just show us the date and not the time component. Since the value is actually a String, the formatting is a bit complex, so we defer to a helper method named as_date.

④ Here, we output the table to the standard output using to_s.

⑤ This is the implementation of as_date, and it simply parses the string from the task and uses strftime (which is named after a UNIX system call that works the same way) to format the date the way we want.

Since neither Todo::Format::Pretty nor Todo::Format::CSV need to do any setup or cleanup, these classes can implement the new methods as no-ops:

break_rules/todo_tables/lib/todo/format/pretty.rb
```
class Pretty
➤   def before; end
➤   def after; end

    # ...

end
```

```
break_rules/todo_tables/lib/todo/format/csv.rb
class CSV
➤  def before; end
➤  def after; end

   # ...

end
```

Now, we make a slight change to the action block of the list command to call our new methods at the right time:

```
break_rules/todo_tables/bin/todo
command :list do |c|

   # ...

     formatter = output_formats[options[:format]]
     File.open(global_options[:filename]) do |tasklist|
➤     formatter.before
       index = 1
       tasks = Todo::TaskBuilder.from_file(tasklist)
       tasks.each do |task|
         formatter.format(index,task)
         index += 1
       end
➤     formatter.after
     end
   end
end
```

We need to do only two more things to make this work. We need to update lib/todo.rb to require our new formatter file, and we need to add it to our list of formatters in the executable.

```
break_rules/todo_tables/lib/todo.rb
require 'todo_version.rb'
require 'todo/task'
require 'todo/format/csv'
require 'todo/format/pretty'
➤ require 'todo/format/table'
```

Thanks to our use of the Strategy pattern that we learned about in Chapter 9, *Be Easy to Maintain*, on page 141, it takes only one line of code to add the new formatter:

```
break_rules/todo_tables/bin/todo
command :list do |c|

   # ...
```

```
  output_formats = {
    'csv' => Todo::Format::CSV.new,
    'pretty' => Todo::Format::Pretty.new,
➤   'table' => Todo::Format::Table.new,
  }
end
```

```
$ bundle exec bin/todo help list
list [command options]
    List tasks
```

```
Command Options:
➤     --format=pretty|table|csv - Format of the output (pretty for
➤                                 TTY, csv otherwise)
      --no-color                - Don't use colors
```

Now when we list our tasks using the "table" format, we get tables, just as expected:

```
$ bundle exec bin/todo list --format=table
+----+---------------------------------------+------------+------------+
| id | name                                  | created    | completed  |
+----+---------------------------------------+------------+------------+
| 1  | Design database schema                | 2011-10-30 |            |
| 2  | Get access to production logs         | 2011-10-30 |            |
| 3  | Code Review                           | 2011-10-30 | 2011-10-30 |
| 4  | Implement model objects for new schema| 2011-10-30 |            |
+----+---------------------------------------+------------+------------+
```

We've talked about nonstandard formatting options for output, but what about input? Most command-line apps accept input from the standard input stream or files, but occasionally we might need an app that allows more user interaction. Such apps are rare, but if you find you need one, Ruby's built-in readline library can allow you to create a sophisticated and easy-to-use user interface.

10.3 Providing Interactive User Input with readline

An interactive user interface, like the one provided by your average SQL client, is a "command-line interface with a command-line app." In other words, this sort of interface provides a customized "shell" into another environment. irb, the Ruby interactive interpreter, is a common example, as are SQL clients. Rather than accept a file full of strings as input, interactive applications provide a command prompt where commands or other input are entered by the user. The user typically has access to a history of commands previously entered and has the ability to edit commands in place before sending them to the program. Also, the user will have the ability to use tab completion of common commands or strings. For example, the MySQL command-line client allows you to tab-complete the names of tables and columns.

Virtually all UNIX applications that provide such an interface use the standard readline library (although some use libedit, which is a replacement and works the same way). Ruby provides bindings for this that make it very easy to use. Keep in mind that it is rare to need to provide such an interface, so let's first talk about when it makes sense.

When to Use an Interactive User Interface

You'll typically want to provide an interactive user interface when your application acts as a gateway into some sort of nonstandard environment. irb is a great example; it allows you to execute arbitrary Ruby code, one command and a time. This sort of interface is especially useful if the expected input is likely to contain characters that are viewed as "special" by the shell. This is one reason why SQL clients use interactive interfaces. The frequent use of asterisks, semicolons, parentheses, and quotes would make it very awkward to enter on a UNIX command line; inside a custom interactive prompt, none of these characters is special and won't need escaping. Further, the ability to control tab completion from within your app can be very useful.

If you aren't making a SQL client or a "Read/Eval/Print Loop" interface to a programming language, it will be unlikely that you'll need to provide an interactive interface. As such, neither db_backup.rb nor todo really lends itself to it, so we'll create a new application to learn the mechanics of doing so using readline.

How to Implement an Interactive Input

Implementing an interactive input, with history browsing and tab completion, is fairly difficult using the various terminal control characters that would be required. Fortunately, the readline C library is widely available on most systems, and the Ruby standard library contains bindings for it so we can access its power from our app.

To learn how to use it, we're going to implement a JSON browser. JSON is a widely used format in web application APIs, something that command-line applications often need to consume. Sophisticated web applications yield heavily nested JSON objects that can be hard to understand by simply viewing them in the terminal. We'll make an interactive application that reads a JSON file from disk and allows the user to move around inside it, inspecting bits of it at time. We'll allow the user to navigate the structure of the JSON data in much the same way a user might navigate a file structure. To make it familiar and easy to learn, we'll use the following commands, closely modeled after similar UNIX commands:

ls

Lists all attributes in the current context

cd xxx

Changes context to the object referenced by the key "xxx"

cd ..

Changes to the context "one up" from where the user is currently

cat xxx

Prints the contents of everything referenced by the key "xxx"

exit

Exits the application

Let's see an example of what we're aiming for. Suppose we have the following JSON file:

break_rules/jb/file.json
```
{
  "result": [
  {
    "name": "Dave",
    "age": 38,
    "state": {
      "name": "Washington, DC",
      "code": "DC"
    }
  },
  {
    "name": "Clay",
    "age": 37,
    "state": {
      "name": "Maryland",
      "code": "MD"
    }
  },
  {
    "name": "Adam",
    "age": 26,
    "state": {
      "name": "California",
      "code": "CA"
    }
  }
  ]
}
```

If we were to run our application on this file, the following session demonstrates the behavior we're looking for:

```
> ls
result
> cd result
> ls
0 1 2
cd 0
> ls
name age state
> cat name
"Dave"
> cd ..
> cd 1
> cd state
> ls
name code
> cat code
"CA"
```

The user also has the ability to use the cursor keys to find old commands and can use tab completion for the cd and cat commands to complete keys available in the current context. This is going to be a much more complex application than we've seen before, and it's all new code, so watch closely.

Bundler has a command, gem, that will provide a rudimentary scaffold for a simple command-line application. We'll call our app jb for "JSON browser" and create it like so:

```
$ bundle gem jb -b
      create   jb/Gemfile
      create   jb/Rakefile
      create   jb/.gitignore
      create   jb/jb.gemspec
      create   jb/lib/jb.rb
      create   jb/lib/jb/version.rb
      create   jb/bin/jb
```

Note that we are using -b, which tells Bundler to create an executable for us. Now that that's set up, we'll add the Ruby library json to our gemspec and run bundle install. Next, we'll need to require both "json" and "readline" at the top of our new executable file, bin/jb (readline is included with Ruby, so we don't need to mention it in our gemspec):

```
break_rules/jb/bin/jb
require 'json'
require 'readline'
require 'optparse'
```

Next, we'll need to set up the basics of our command-line interface. We don't need any options, so things are pretty minimal:

```
break_rules/jb/bin/jb
option_parser = OptionParser.new do |opts|
  executable_name = File.basename($PROGRAM_NAME)
  opts.banner = "Interactively browse a JSON file

Usage: #{executable_name} json_file"
end

option_parser.parse!

json_file = ARGV.shift
if json_file && File.exists?(json_file)
  main(json_file)
else
  STDERR.puts "error: you must provide a JSON file as an argument"
  exit 1
end
```

You'll notice that we still use OptionParser even though we have no options. This gives us --help for free and provides an easy way to add options later. You'll also notice that we're calling a main method. We'll see that next, as we move onto the meat of the program.

The way readline works is very simple. We call the method readline on the class Readline, which provides the interactive prompt and returns us the string that the user entered. The readline method takes two arguments: a String, representing the prompt to show the user, and a boolean that, if true, will instruct Readline to store the history so the user can use their cursor keys to scroll back through the command history. Here's the basic loop we'll run to get the commands the user typed:

```
break_rules/jb/bin/jb
def main(json_file)
  root = JSON.parse(File.read(json_file))
  command = nil

  while command != 'exit'
    command = Readline.readline("> ",true)
    break if command.nil?
    # execute the command
  end
end
```

The first thing we do is parse the JSON file using the JSON library's JSON.parse method. File.read returns the contents of a file as a string, and parse returns a

Hash with the parsed JSON. After that, we enter a loop that uses Readline to get the user's input. The readline method returns whatever the user typed at the prompt. If the user hit CTRL-D (which is the control character for "end of file" and indicates the user wants to exit), null is returned, so we break out in that case. Next, we need to handle an actual command, which will require us to determine a way to navigate up and down the tree of the parsed JSON.

We'll do this by using a nested structure that records where we are in the Hash. This structure, called a Context, will have a reference to the current location and to a parent Context. This way, we can easily traverse back up when a user enters cd ... Here's part of the class:

break_rules/jb/bin/jb
```
class Context
  attr_reader :here
  attr_reader :parent_context

  def initialize(here,parent_context)
    @here = here
    @parent_context = parent_context
  end
end
```

Next, we'll initialize the root context in main and defer all command-handling duties to a method called execute_command, which takes the current context as an argument and returns the new context resulting from whatever command was executed:

break_rules/jb/bin/jb
```
def main(json_file)
  root = JSON.parse(File.read(json_file))
  command = nil

➤ current_context = Context.new(root,nil)

  while command != 'exit'
    command = Readline.readline("> ",true)
    break if command.nil?
    # execute the command
➤   current_context = execute_command(command.strip,current_context)
  end
end
```

Next, we'll implement execute_command. This method will use a case statement to match on the known commands. Each when clause will handle one command by passing it to the current_context (which, you'll recall, is an instance of Context). Note the highlighted methods in Context that we're assuming exist.

break_rules/jb/bin/jb

```ruby
def execute_command(command,current_context)
  case command
  when /^ls$/
➤    puts current_context.to_s
  when /^cd (.*$)/
➤    new_context = current_context.cd($1)
    if new_context.nil?
      puts "No such key #{$1}"
    else
      current_context = new_context
    end
  when /^cat (.*)$/
➤    item = current_context.cat($1)
    if item.nil?
      puts "No such item #{$1}"
    else
      puts item.inspect
    end
  when /^help$/
    puts "cat <item> - print the contents of <item> in the current context"
    puts "cd  <item> - change context to the context of <item>"
    puts "cd  ..     - change up one level"
    puts "ls         - list available items in the current context"
  end
  current_context
end
```

As you can see, we've assumed that the methods cd, to_s, and cat exist on Context. We'll see those in a minute, but we've assumed that cd and cat return nil if anything goes wrong, and we message the user in this case. Note that we're *not* using the standard error here. Since we're interacting with the user, there's no other output than the results of the user's actions, so it's simplest to use the standard output stream for everything. We've also included a help command, since we want our app to be helpful (as we learned in Chapter 3, *Be Helpful*, on page 33).

We'll start off with to_s, which will check the type of here and transform it into the list of keys to which the user can cd:

break_rules/jb/bin/jb

```ruby
def to_s
  if self.here.kind_of? Array
    indices = []
    self.here.each_index { |i| indices << i }
    indices.join(' ')
  elsif self.here.kind_of? Hash
    self.here.keys.join(' ')
  else
```

```
      self.here.to_s
    end
  end
end
```

cat and cd are both very simple, relying on a private method item_at, which handles accessing the item inside here that matches path, the parameter to both cat and cd:

break_rules/jb/bin/jb
```
def cat(path)
  item_at(path)
end

def cd(path)
  if path == '..'
    self.parent_context
  else
    item = item_at(path)
    if item.nil?
      nil
    else
      Context.new(item,self)
    end
  end
end
private

def item_at(path)
  if path == '..'
    self.parent_context.here
  elsif self.here.kind_of? Array
    self.here[path.to_i]
  elsif self.here.kind_of? Hash
    self.here[path]
  else
    nil
  end
end
```

That's a lot of code, but it'll make it easy to add tab completion to our app, which we're going to do next. First, let's see this version in action:

```
$ bundle exec bin/jb file.json
> ls
result
> cd result
> ls
0 1 2
> cd 99
No such key 99
> cd 1
```

```
> ls
name age state
> cat name
"Clay"
> cd ..
> cat 0
{"name"=>"Dave", "age"=>38, "state"=>{"name"=>"Washington, DC", "code"=>"DC"}}
> exit
```

Everything works great! Now, let's allow the user to tab-complete the keys available when using the cd or cat command. To do this, we register a Proc with Readline that, when executed, will be given the current input as a string and expects an Array of possible completions as a result. To set it up, we call completion_proc= on Readline:

break_rules/jb_completion/bin/jb
```
def main(json_file)
  root = JSON.parse(File.read(json_file))
  command = nil

  current_context = Context.new(root,nil)

➤  Readline.completion_proc = proc { |input|
➤    current_context.completions(input)
➤  }

  while command != 'exit'
    command = Readline.readline("> ",true)
    break if command.nil?
    current_context = execute_command(command.strip,current_context)
  end
end
```

Our Proc is simply sending the input to a new method of Context called completions. Since the list of completions is essentially the same as the output of ls, we'll use the to_s method to get a list of completions:

break_rules/jb_completion/bin/jb
```
class Context

  # ...

  def completions(input)
    self.to_s.split(/\s+/).grep(/^#{input}/)
  end

end
```

Here, we split the output of to_s on a space and then use the method grep, available on all Array instances, to trim out only what matches the input. This way, if we have a JSON object with the keys "dave," "dan," and "amy" and the user types "da" and hits TAB, the user will see only "dave" and "dan" as possible completions. Let's try it:

```
bundle exec bin/jb file.json
> cd res<TAB>
> cd result
> cd<TAB>
0  1  2
> cd 1
> cat na<TAB>
> cat name
"Clay"
> exit
```

If you can try this on your computer, it will be easier to see how it works, but you can tab-complete just as you can in your shell. Since the completion algorithm is entirely under your control, you can make it as sophisticated as you like.

10.4 Moving On

This brings us to the end of our journey. We've come a long way from using OptionParser to parse the command line. We can now provide sophisticated help text, integrate with any other system or command, and distribute our code to any environment, all while keeping our app tested and maintainable. As we learned in this chapter, we can even spruce it up with sophisticated input and output, if the need should arise.

So, what's left? The techniques we've learned are applicable to your everyday tasks and can be applied to any command-line app you need to write. We've also learned some handy tools and libraries; however, these only scratch the surface. The great thing about the Ruby community is the wide variety of tools available to solve problems. If you thought OptionParser was too verbose or you didn't like the way your command suite looked using GLI, never fear; there's more than one way to do it. In the appendix that follows, we'll take a quick tour of some other popular command-line libraries and show you how our running examples, db_backup and todo, might look using tools like Thor, Main, and Trollop.

Common Command-Line
Gems and Libraries

To keep things simple, we've used only a handful of tools to demonstrate the principles presented in this book. We chose OptionParser because it's a standard library available with Ruby, and we used GLI because of the ease with which we can add the necessary features of a command suite.

Since Ruby allows such a wide variety in programming style, it should be no surprise that there are many different libraries for writing command-line apps, each with its own unique style. We'll go over a few popular libraries that exhibit different styles of writing a command-line app. You might find some of them more suited to the way you prefer to work, but the goal is always the same: to make awesome command-line apps easily and quickly, using whatever tools work best for you. Also keep in mind that there are many more libraries available than we have time to look at, but these are tools you're likely to see in the real world.

This appendix is split up into three major sections. In the first, we'll show some alternative implementations of our simple command-line app db_backup.rb using three alternatives to OptionParser: trollop, methadone, and main. In the second section, we'll do the same thing with our command suite todo, using thor and main. The final section will be a whirlwind tour of the tools we couldn't cover and where you can find out more about them.

Since, by now, you should be well familiar with the problems that db_backup.rb and todo solve, we'll show a lot more code at once. For each library, we'll outline its general design and features, show the implementation using that library (possibly calling out interesting or confusing bits of code), and conclude with a brief discussion of its pros and cons.

A1.1 Alternatives for Simple Command-Line Apps

We saw in Chapter 2, *Be Easy to Use*, on page 13 and Chapter 3, *Be Helpful*, on page 33 that OptionParser is very powerful, particularly in the way in which its on method works. If we don't need this power, however, OptionParser can feel a bit verbose. Often, all we want to do is have the existence/absence of flags and switches populate a Hash, like so:

```
opts.on("-u USER","--username","Database user") do |username|
  options[:username] = username
end
```

This can get tedious and add unnecessary complexity to our code. Because of this, several libraries have been developed to make this simpler. We'll look at three different libraries that try to solve this problem and make it easier for you to specify your command-line interface.

trollop

trollop[1] aims to allow parsing command-line options with as little code as possible. Instead of using the three lines per option that we've seen thus far, trollop allows you to specify options in one line. It doesn't use OptionParser internally and supports only a subset of its features.

trollop has two modes of operation. In the simplest mode, you make a call to Trollop::options, which takes a block. That block defines your user interface (which we'll see in a bit) and returns a Hash of the options the user provided on the command line. In the second mode, these two activities are split into two steps. You first declare your user interface by passing a block to Trollop::Parser.new, which returns a parser object. You then use that parser to parse the command line by calling parse, which returns a Hash of the command-line options.

For db_backup.rb, we have to use the second form, since we are reading defaults from an external config file. Unlike OptionParser, trollop does not provide direct access to the Hash of options beforehand. Instead, we'll apply our defaults after parsing. There is a second advantage to this mode as well.

trollop provides a method Trollop::with_standard_exception_handling, which takes a block. Certain exceptions, if thrown inside this block, will kick off trollop's default error handling. In addition to calling parse inside this block (since parse throws trollop-specific exceptions), we'll also look for our default argument, the database name, and throw Trollop::HelpNeeded if we don't find it. This replaces

---

1. http://trollop.rubyforge.org/

our explicit exit and call to to_s on OptionParser from our original implementation. Let's see what the code looks like at this point:

```
cli_tools_roundup/db_backup/trollop/bin/db_backup.rb
parser = Trollop::Parser.new do

  # declare UI...

end

options = Trollop::with_standard_exception_handling(parser) do
  o = parser.parse(ARGV)
➤ defaults.each do |key,val|
➤   o[key] = val if o[key].nil?
➤ end
  if ARGV.empty?
    STDERR.puts "error: you must supply a database name"
    raise Trollop::HelpNeeded
  end
  o
end
```

The highlighted code is where we apply our defaults from the config file (it's parsed the same as before). Only if the user didn't specify something on the command line do we apply the default.

With this basic structure, how do we declare our UI? Trollop provides the method opt, which handles this for us. To declare our --username flag, which also responds to -u, we need just one line of code:

```
cli_tools_roundup/db_backup/trollop/bin/db_backup.rb
opt :username, "Database username, in first.last format", :type => :string
```

trollop will automatically assign a short-form option based on the first letter of the long-form option. Further, by specifying the :type => :string option, we indicate that this is a flag. If we used something like :int instead, trollop would convert the type for us.

In the case of our switch --end-of-iteration, we want the short form to be -i and not the -e that trollop would pick by default. We can change this using the :long option, like so:

```
cli_tools_roundup/db_backup/trollop/bin/db_backup.rb
opt :i, 'Indicate that this backup is an "iteration" backup',
  :long => 'end-of-iteration'
```

There's a slight bit of complication with the option parsing because trollop doesn't support negatable options. In the OptionParser version, we used a string like "--[no-]gzip to accept both --gzip and --no-gzip. Although trollop doesn't support this, we can simulate it using two options and the conflict method, like so:

```
cli_tools_roundup/db_backup/trollop/bin/db_backup.rb
opt 'no-gzip',"Do not compress the backup file", :default => false
opt :gzip,"Compress the backup file", :default => true
conflicts(:gzip,'no-gzip')
```

If the user specifies both options, they will get an error, and we still have the fluent user interface that we want. The rest of our code is largely the same after option parsing; we have a Hash named options that contains the command-line options the user provided.

We've seen how trollop eliminates a lot of boilerplate needed in declaring the user interface. trollop is also designed to be distributed as a single file you can include in your application for distribution; this can be a huge advantage in environments where installing external dependencies is difficult or impossible.

So, if you are doing something idiomatic with OptionParser, trollop can save you quite a bit of code. The trade-off comes from a few missing features. trollop does not provide validation via a regexp, Array, or Hash, nor does it support OptionParser's flexible type conversions. Still, trollop can be a time-saver for simpler apps that you want to implement quickly, where you might not need all of OptionParser's power to get the job done.

methadone

methadone[2] was developed by the author while writing this book. Like trollop, its goal is to reduce the amount of code you have to write to parse the command line. Unlike trollop, however, methadone still provides access to all of OptionParser's features. Further, methadone handles several other time-consuming tasks when writing a command-line application, such as the following:

* Bootstrap your application, providing a .gemspec, Rakefile, README, a unit test, and an acceptance test with one easy command.

* Place main logic at the top of your file in a "main" method, instead of at the bottom where it's hard to find.

* Automatically create the banner based on the UI you've declared.

Unlike trollop, methadone doesn't provide its own command-line parsing; it's simply a proxy to OptionParser, along with a few helper methods. Let's talk about the helper methods first, since they define the structure of your executable's

---

2.   https://github.com/davetron5000/methadone

source code. All of methadone's helper methods and features can be brought into your app by including the Methadone::Main module. Immediately after that, make a call to the main method, which takes a block.

This block should be the logic of your application. It can access the parsed command-line options via the variable options, which is a simple Hash. Command-line arguments will be passed into the block, so define your block to accept whatever arguments you need. The block given to main is executed when you call another helper method, go!. go! parses the command line and then calls your block with the remaining unparsed command-line arguments. It handles exceptions thrown from your block, messaging the user and exiting accordingly, as well as effectively replacing the begin/rescue code we were using in the original db_backup.rb. The structure is as follows:

cli_tools_roundup/db_backup/methadone/bin/db_backup.rb
```
include Methadone::Main

main do |database_name|

  # main logic of the app...

end

# define any helper methods here...

# declare user interface here

go!
```

Between our call to main and our call to go!, we can declare our user interface. Because we've included Methadone::Main, we have access to the variable opts, which is an instance of OptionParser. We could then declare options as normal, like so:

```
main do |database_name|

  # main logic of the app...

end

opts.on("-u USER","--username",
        "Database username, in first.last format") do |username|
  options[:username] = username
end

# ...

go!
```

methadone provides a helper method to make this idiomatic use of OptionParser more compact. The on method accepts all of the same arguments as the on method of OptionParser, but it takes care of extracting the value and placing it in the options hash. The following code is identical to the call to opts.on shown earlier:

```
cli_tools_roundup/db_backup/methadone/bin/db_backup.rb
on('-u USER','--username','Database username, in first.last format')
```

Since opts is just an OptionParser, we could create our banner as normal; however, methadone takes care of this for us. We simply need to provide the missing bits of information, which can be done via the description and arg helper methods:

```
cli_tools_roundup/db_backup/methadone/bin/db_backup.rb
description "Backup one or more MySQL databases"

arg :database_name, :required, :many
```

arg also does a bit of sanity checking for us. Since we've declared our argument as :required, methadone will raise an error if this is omitted on the command line.

As for using our external configuration for defaults, methadone doesn't support this directly, so, as with trollop, we have to do things a bit more manually. Since methadone creates the options hash, we have to slightly change how we configure it with our defaults, and we then have to explicitly set the defaults from the config file, as shown here:

```
cli_tools_roundup/db_backup/methadone/bin/db_backup.rb
➤ options[:gzip] = true
➤ options[:force] = false
➤ options['end-of-iteration'] = false
➤ options[:username] = nil
➤ options[:password] = nil

  CONFIG_FILE = File.join(ENV['HOME'],'.db_backup.rc.yaml')

  if File.exists? CONFIG_FILE
    options_config = YAML.load_file(CONFIG_FILE)
➤   options_config.each do |key,val|
➤     options[key] = val
➤   end
  else
    File.open(CONFIG_FILE,'w') { |file| YAML::dump(options,file) }
    warn "Initialized configuration file in #{CONFIG_FILE}"
  end

  # now declare user interface
```

methadone removes quite a bit of boilerplate when using OptionParser in an idiomatic way but, since it's just a proxy, still allows you complete access to everything that OptionParser can do. For many common command-line apps, this can cut down on a lot of code and let you get things up and running much more quickly. methadone also provides some additional Cucumber steps that can be used with Aruba to get better test coverage of your app.

Like trollop, however, we no longer have easy access to a Hash of options to manipulate, and methadone provides no assistance with our external configuration. Unlike trollop, methadone is available only as a gem, so any app that uses it will need the methadone gem installed.

main

main[3] describes itself as "a class factory and DSL for generating command-line programs real quick." It is designed around unifying all input to your app, be it arguments, command-line options, or environment variables, and it provides an easy-to-understand, if verbose, syntax for describing your command-line interface.

When declaring your user interface with main, you indicate where each bit of input you require will come from, and main handles retrieving it from the right place. You can then access it all from the variable params, and your code doesn't need to worry about *where* a particular bit of information came from. main will also generate documentation appropriate to these sources, which can be very handy if your app responds to environment variables. As we'll see, this gives you exactly one way to access user input, which can serve to make your code more readable and extensible.

First let's see the general outline of how db_backup.rb would like using main. Our entire app's code goes into a block that's given to the method Main. Inside this block, we can declare the options, arguments, and other input. Then, we call the method run, which takes a block containing the app's main logic. Inside this block, params is available to provide access to any value the user provided as input, be it from options, the environment, or command-line arguments. Here's the basic overview:

cli_tools_roundup/db_backup/main/bin/db_backup.rb
```
require 'main'

Main {

  # declare options and arguments
```

---

3. https://github.com/ahoward/main

```
run {
  auth = ""
  auth += "-u#{params['username'].value} " if params['username'].value
  auth += "-p#{params['password'].value} " if params['password'].value

  database_name = params['database_name'].value

  # rest of the main logic...

}
}
```

One thing to note is that params isn't just a hash of the option values but a hash that maps the option names to instances of Main::Parameter. Instances of this class provide the method value, which provides the value provided by the user.

Next, we need to declare our user interface. main takes a different approach than methadone or trollop. Instead of trying to condense everything into one line of code, main provides a detailed, readable format. Inside the block given to Main, the methods option, argument, and environment allow you to declare an input to your program. These all take a block in which various methods can be called to describe the aspects of the input. Let's look at one of our more complex options, --username:

cli_tools_roundup/db_backup/main/bin/db_backup.rb
```
option('username') {
  description 'Database username, in first.last format'
  argument :required
  default options[:username]
  validate do |arg|
    arg =~ /^[^\.]+\.[^\.]+$/
  end
}
```

Each line of code tells main one piece of information about the option. description is used to generate help text, argument allows us to specify that the flag's argument is optional (or not), and default indicates the default value. Here, we've used the value option[:username], which we read from our external configuration, as the default value. main uses this in a manner similar to GLI, in that the default value will appear in documentation but will also be returned by params as the value if the user omits it from the command line.

Last in our block to option is the validate method, which takes a block. This block is given the value from the command line, and if the block evaluates to true, the option is accepted. Otherwise, it is rejected, and main will exit your app with an error. Since it takes a block, it's a bit more powerful than Option-Parser, although it's slightly more verbose for simple cases.

You may have noticed that main provides only the method option, and not one for flags and another for switches. main treats these the same, so to accept a switch, we simply omit the argument call, as we've done here for our "end-of-iteration" switch:

cli_tools_roundup/db_backup/main/bin/db_backup.rb
```
option('end-of-iteration') {
  description 'Mark this as an "end-of-iteration" backup'
  default options[:'end-of-iteration']
}
```

You should also be aware that main does not support short-form options. Even if we declare the name of an option to be a single character, main will require it to be passed with two dashes (e.g., option('i') requires --i on the command line). Also, main doesn't support negatable options, so we must declare both --gzip and --no-gzip separately, as we did with trollop.

As we mentioned, main allows you to specify arguments to your command-line app in the same fashion as with options. This turns out to be fairly handy, since main will check for required arguments, document them, and provide access to them via params. Here's how we declare our single argument, database_name:

cli_tools_roundup/db_backup/main/bin/db_backup.rb
```
argument('database_name') {
  description 'database to backup'
  argument :required
}
```

This looks similar in structure to our use of option and exemplifies main's unified way of describing and accessing user input. When the user runs our app, params['database_name'].value will provide the value the user specified on the command line.

Despite main's limitations, the unified access is a useful design. It means we can change around where values come from, and it won't affect our main logic. This can be quite handy when first developing your app, since you might not have a good sense of what should be a flag and what should be an argument. It's also worth pointing out that main's verbosity can be an advantage. Users unfamiliar with your app, or the tools used to create its UI, will more easily understand the code for a main-powered app than for one using trollop or methadone. If you happen to be the author of an internal command-line app that's being used other developers or sysadmins, it can be very nice when they can enhance the app themselves, instead of bothering you for changes.

main, like trollop and methadone, is actively maintained. All three are fine alternatives to OptionParser, so use the one that feels right for you whenever you're writing a simple command-line app.

In the next section, we'll look at alternatives for making a command suite. We'll see how main works well for these as well, and we'll also look at thor, which is a popular tool for making command suites, as well as a library for making Ruby on Rails generators.

A1.2 Alternatives for Command Suites

We saw how GLI provides us with the tools to make an awesome command suite, but, like with OptionParser, you might want to do things differently. You may want to provide a much simpler application with less code, sacrificing some power for quicker delivery. In this case, thor is an excellent choice. You may, instead, not want to use a different tool for simple apps as you do for command suites. In this case, main is a good choice, especially if you are transitioning a simple app to a command suite. We'll look at both of them here by reimplementing todo using each library.

main

Since we just looked at main in the previous section, let's stay with it and see how it works for command suites. You may have noticed that the way in which GLI works is vastly different from how OptionParser works. main takes the complete opposite approach and works very similarly for both regular apps and command suites. main refers to commands as *modes* and provides the method mode to declare them. First let's see how we declare our global options. It's done just like with a simple app: inside the Main block:

```
cli_tools_roundup/todo/main/bin/todo
Main {
  option('filename') {
    description "Path to the todo file"
    argument :required
    default File.join(ENV['HOME'],'.todo.txt')
  }

  mode 'list' do

    # declare options and logic for the list mode/command

  end
```

Inside our mode block, we can declare options and arguments specific to that mode/command, like so:

```
cli_tools_roundup/todo/main/bin/todo
mode 'list' do
  description 'List tasks'
  output_formats = {
    'csv' => Todo::Format::CSV,
    'pretty' => Todo::Format::Pretty,
  }
  option('format') {
    description 'Format of the output (pretty for TTY, csv otherwise)'
    argument :required
  }
  run {
    format = params['format'].value
    if format.nil?
      if STDOUT.tty?
        format = 'pretty'
      else
        format = 'csv'
      end
    end

    formatter = output_formats[format]
    File.open(params['filename'].value) do |tasklist|
      index = 1
      tasks = Todo::TaskBuilder.from_file(tasklist)
      tasks.each do |task|
        formatter.format(index,task)
        index += 1
      end
    end
  }
end
```

The contents of our run block are pretty much the same as in the action block of the GLI version. The implementations of new and done are similar. One big difference in the main version of todo and the one we created using GLI is in how the user interface acts.

For example, there's no formal differentiation between global and command-specific options. Global options can be specified anywhere on the command line and share the same namespace with command-specific options. If you'll recall, todo used -f, when a global option, to indicate the to-do filename and used it as a command-specific option to new to indicate that the next task should be placed first in the tasklist. Since main doesn't allow short-form options, this isn't a problem in this case, but it's a limitation to be aware of.

Although main provides a two-level help system, like the one we described in Chapter 3, *Be Helpful*, on page 33, it works in a slightly different fashion than the help provided by most command suites. In a main-powered app, you get help for a command by issuing the -h or --help option or by giving it the argument help, like so:

```
$ bin/todo list --help
NAME
  todo

SYNOPSIS
  todo list [options]+

DESCRIPTION
  List tasks

PARAMETERS
  --force-tty
  --filename=filename (0 ~> filename=/Users/davec/.todo.txt)
      Path to the todo file
  --format=format (0 ~> format)
      Format of the output (pretty for TTY, csv otherwise)
  --help, -h
$ bin/todo list help
# => produces the same output
```

main also doesn't have direct support for external config files, like GLI does, so we'd need to read them in "by hand" as we've been doing in our simple command-line apps. Despite these limitations and nonstandard behavior, there's a real advantage to using only one tool for all of your command-line apps. Aside from having to be knowledgeable in only a single tool, it's also easy to transform a simple app into a command suite. Just add the necessary calls to mode.

thor

thor[4] is a library created by Yehuda Katz that, among other things, provides an easy way to make simple command-suite applications. thor also provides other features, such as support for Rails generators and the ability to install and manage tasks in your system, but it's the command-suite support we're interested in. thor is not as feature-filled as GLI but requires a lot less code to get a command suite up and running and can be very handy for getting something out quickly.

---

4. https://github.com/wycats/thor

The thor gem provides a base class, Thor, that you extend to create your command suite. The methods of your subclass are the commands in your suite, with the arguments to those methods being their command-line arguments. Subclassing the Thor base class also provides access to several helper "macro"-style methods to let you describe your app and its commands, as well as define arguments. Thor provides the method start, which kicks off your app. Here's the skeleton of a thor-powered app:

cli_tools_roundup/todo/thor/bin/todo
```
require 'thor'

class TodoApp < Thor

  # declare global options and commands...

end

TodoApp.start
```

To declare global options, use the method class_option, which takes a string or symbol as the primary option name and then a hash of options. Here's how we declare the global option for --filename, which declares where todo will find the task list:

cli_tools_roundup/todo/thor/bin/todo
```
class_option :f, :aliases => ['--filename'],
                 :default => File.join(ENV['HOME'],'.todo.txt'),
                 :desc => "Location of the todo.txt file",
                 :banner => 'FILE'
```

The options do what they appear to do:

:aliases

    This is a list of alternate forms for the option.

:default

    This is the default value for the option, which is used both for documentation and to provide the default value in code when the user omits this option on the command line.

:desc

    This is the description of the option, used to generate help text.

:banner

    This is similar to GLI's arg_name method; it is used to generate help text and name the argument accepted by this option.

To define a command, we simply define a method. The name of the method is the name of the command, and the name and number of arguments are the name and number of arguments to that command. To describe the command and define command-specific options, the methods desc and method_option are called *before* we define our method. Here's how we'd define the new command:

```
cli_tools_roundup/todo/thor/bin/todo
method_option :first, :default => false,
                      :desc => "Put the new task at the top of the list",
                      :type => :boolean
method_option :p, :aliases => ['--priority'],
                  :desc => "Set the priority of the option",
                  :banner => 'priority'
desc "new task_names...", "New todo"
def new(*task_names)
  if task_names.empty?
    puts "Reading new tasks from stdin..."
    task_names = STDIN.readlines.map { |a| a.chomp }
  end
  Todo::Task.new_task(options['f'],task_names)
end
```

Note that, like main, thor makes no formal distinction between flags and switches. Here, we indicate that --first is a switch by using the :type option, with a value of :boolean. The values of our options will be available inside our methods via the options hash.

Note the format of the arguments to desc. The first argument is the invocation syntax (e.g., todo new task_names...), and the second argument is used for help text. Also, note that we're using the "splat" style for our argument to the new method. This tells thor that new takes multiple arguments. If we'd omitted the asterisk and defined our method like def new(task_name), thor would notice that and accept only one argument.

As you can see, thor is incredibly simple. This simplicity comes at a trade-off, however. As with main, all options share a common namespace, meaning that we cannot have a global -f and an -f specific to new. This also affects the command-line invocation syntax. To invoke an app that uses thor, *all* switches and flags must come at the *end* of the command line. Consider this command-line invocation of todo that adds a task to a custom task list:

`$ bin/todo --filename=/tmp/foo.txt new "Take out trash"`

Our GLI version would add the new task to the file /tmp/foo.txt. The thor version prints out the help text and exits zero. If we move the option after the command, things get a bit more confusing:

```
$ bin/todo new --filename=/tmp/foo.txt "Take out trash"
Reading new tasks from stdin...
^D
```

thor views anything between the command name and the first option as the arguments. In this invocation, there is nothing between them, so task_names is empty in our new method, which kicks off the alternate flow to read tasks from the standard input. The correct invocation for our thor-powered app is as follows:

```
$ bin/todo new "Take out trash" --filename=/tmp/foo.txt
```

This may seem like a serious trade-off since thor apps don't behave like common command suites, but don't forget how simple thor is to use. If you need to whip up a basic command suite, thor makes it very easy, since you just need to make a class with a few methods in it.

A1.3 Other Relevant Libraries

As we mentioned, the tools we saw here are just a small part of the libraries available for writing command-line apps in Ruby. In this section, we'll list some more that we don't have space to delve into but that are still worth checking out.

Command-Line Parsers

We've seen a few command-line parsers already, but there are many more you can use. Many of these are similar to the tools we've seen, but they all have their own individual style and features, so if none of what we've seen really grabs you, please check these out:

choice (https://github.com/defunkt/choice)
> choice is a command-line parser for simple command-line apps that has a syntax similar to main. It provides typecasting, validation, automatic documentation, and all the other things you'd expect of a command-line parser.

commander (https://github.com/visionmedia/commander)
> commander can be used to create a command suite and has a very similar syntax to GLI.

cri (https://github.com/ddfreyne/cri)
> cri is a command-line parser that can create a simple command-line app or a command suite and uses a syntax that is a mix of main and GLI. Unlike

these libraries, cri has support for nested commands, allowing for an invocation syntax like my_app command sub_command subsub_command args.

Mixlib-CLI (https://github.com/opscode/mixlib-cli)
Mixlib-CLI is maintained by Opscode, which maintains the popular chef system maintenance tool. Mixlib-CLI is for creating simple command-line apps and has a syntax similar to main, in that it is verbose yet readable.

optitron (https://github.com/joshbuddy/optitron)
optitron is for making command suites and has a syntax similar to thor. optitron provides more validation of options and arguments and has a concise syntax for naming command-line arguments and documenting their defaults, via extracting the Ruby code for the methods that back the commands.

slop (https://github.com/injekt/slop)
slop allows you to create simple command-line apps and has a syntax very similar to trollop. slop provides more validations and more features than you might find in OptionParser. slop also defaults switches to allow negative versions (e.g., --no-switch), which, as we know, makes for a more fluent user interface.

Libraries for Fancy User Interfaces

In Chapter 10, *Add Color, Formatting, and Interactivity*, on page 153, we used terminal-table and rainbow to create a nonstandard user interface. Here are some additional tools that work differently or provide additional features, such as progress bars:

formatador (https://github.com/geemus/formatador)
formatador is a general-purpose library for producing rich output to a terminal. It uses an HTML-like syntax to produce colored output but can also do some basic formatting such as indentation and overwriting (where a line of output is replaced without a linefeed moving it up one line). formatador can also display ASCII tables and progress bars.

highline (https://github.com/JEG2/highline)
highline is a library for interacting with the user in a question-and-answer format (as opposed to readline, which is a full interactive prompt). You request input from the user by calling ask and can give the user output via the method say. There is support for type conversions and validation. This is an excellent library if your app must interact with the user to figure out what to do.

paint (https://github.com/janlelis/paint)

> paint allows you to produce colored output to the terminal, but, unlike rainbow, paint does not monkey-patch String. It provides a simple method, Paint, that handles everything. paint also allows you to specify your colors using RGB instead of simple names like "green." This is handy for terminals that support 256 colors.

progress_bar (https://github.com/paul/progress_bar)

> progress_bar produces a progress bar in the terminal, complete with a percentage and an elapsed time.

term-ansicolor (https://github.com/flori/term-ansicolor)

> term-ansicolor is another library for producing colored output to the terminal. Unlike rainbow and paint, which color and style strings, term-ansicolor provides methods that turn colors and styles on and off, with a method clear that resets everything. This is closer to how the ANSI color codes actually work.

Testing Libraries Useful for Command-Line Apps

We've seen aruba and mocha for help in testing our command-line apps, but there are many other libraries for helping to test your application. Here are a few that are most useful when writing command-line apps:

construct (https://github.com/devver/construct)

> construct allows you to create temporary directory structures and files specifically for testing. This can be handy if your app is expecting to work within some sort of directory hierarchy. Instead of manipulating the actual system files, you can use construct to set things up for any situation you want to test, and everything gets cleaned up after your tests run.

FakeFS (https://github.com/defunkt/fakefs)

> FakeFS is similar to construct, in that it allows you to manipulate files during testing. FakeFS replaces Ruby's internal file classes with its own and is somewhat more limited but can run faster since it doesn't interact with the filesystem.

This concludes our whirlwind tour of alternatives for writing command-line apps. Our intention wasn't to show you every library and tool there is but to demonstrate the wide variety of styles available in some of the more popular libraries. If you'd like to learn about more tools, try searching in github.com or rubygems.org to discover new libraries.

Bibliography

[Bec02]   Kent Beck. *Test Driven Development: By Example*. Addison-Wesley, Reading, MA, 2002.

[CADH09] David Chelimsky, Dave Astels, Zach Dennis, Aslak Hellesøy, Bryan Helmkamp, and Dan North. *The RSpec Book*. The Pragmatic Bookshelf, Raleigh, NC and Dallas, TX, 2009.

[GHJV95] Erich Gamma, Richard Helm, Ralph Johnson, and John Vlissides. *Design Patterns: Elements of Reusable Object-Oriented Software*. Addison-Wesley, Reading, MA, 1995.

[Swi08]   Travis Swicegood. *Pragmatic Version Control Using Git*. The Pragmatic Bookshelf, Raleigh, NC and Dallas, TX, 2008.

[TFH09]   David Thomas, Chad Fowler, and Andrew Hunt. *Programming Ruby: The Pragmatic Programmer's Guide*. The Pragmatic Bookshelf, Raleigh, NC and Dallas, TX, Third Edition, 2009.

Index

A

accept method, on OptionParser, 24

acceptance tests
  installing Cucumber and Aruba, 121–123
  running Cucumber tests, 123–124
  testing complex behavior, 125–127
  testing execution of external commands, 127–131
  understanding, 118–119
  understanding Cucumber and Aruba, 119–121
  using, 118–131

ack, use of color, 154–155

After method, 126

ANSI escape sequences, adding color using ANSI escape sequences, 155–159

ARGF class, 80

arguments
  command-line, 15–16
  default value for app, 79–82
  documenting command line arguments, 35–36
  expected use case of ls, 82
  to flags, controlling output formatting, 78–79
  to flags, documenting, 49
  to trap signals from other apps, 69
  using ellipsis for multiple, 48

using square bracket ([]) syntax, 48
validating to flags, 22–23

ARGV
  as command, 8
  checking, 38
  using as Array, 3

Array, using ARGV as, 38

Array of Symbol, passing to command, 76

Arrays
  in OptionParser, 24
  using ARGV, 3

Aruba
  installing, 121–123
  modifying values to run, 126
  operating systems that support, 122
  understanding, 119, 121

as_date method, 162

AUTHOR section, meaning of, 51

automating specialized tasks, 2–5

awesome command-line apps, overview of, 10–11

awk command, in UNIX, 66–67

B

backing up data app
  accessing standard output and error streams, 60–61
  avoiding destructive behavior in, 83–84
  building with OptionParser, 19–23

choosing option names, 72–75
determining if process succeeded, 54–59
documenting, command line arguments, 35–36
external configuration of, 90–94
including man page in, 42–47
purpose of, 36
simplifying app, 2–5
testing execution of external commands, 127–130
trapping signals from other apps, 68–69
using main as alternative to OptionParser, 181–184
using methadone as alternative to OptionParser, 179–181
using trollop as alternative to OptionParser, 176–178
writing README file for, 112–114

backtick operator ('), 60

banner, 35, 37, 47

basename method, 36

bash, vii, 30, 55

Beck, Kent, 139

Before method, 126

begin..rescue..end construct, 58

bit-shifting, 58

BUGS section, meaning of, 51

Bugzilla, 5

build-automation tools, Ruby's, 104

bundle exec, 144, 164, 171, 173

bundler
about, 17
command gem, 167
creation of, 110–111
installing color using, 155–159
updating gems with, 121–123

C

capture3 method, 60

case statements, 8–10, 169

cat xxx command, 166

cd xxx command, 166

cd.. command, 166

choice, 189

classes, encapsulating data and code into classes, 147

classnames, in OptionParser argument list, 23

code
designing for maintainability, 146–151
encapsulating into classes, 147

code organization, dividing code into multiple files, 141–146

collaborating, with other developers, 109–115

color
about using color, 154–155
adding color using ANSI escape sequences, 155–159
benefits of using, 153

color blindness, using color and, 155

comma-separated-values format, 7

command method, passing Array of Symbol to, 76

command suites
about, 8
alternatives to using, 184–186
choosing names in command suites, 75–76
defining parts of, 16–18
documenting, 38–42

documenting commands in, 49
format for documentation, 48
naming commands in, 17

command-line
arguments, 15–16
options, 14–15
parts of command-line app invocation, 15
understanding parts of, 13–18

command-line apps
about, 1
adding descriptions, 36–38
overview of awesome, 10–11
using git, 16

command-line interface, documenting, 33–38

command-specific options (command options), 17

command-suite interface, building with GLI, 23–31

commander, 189
open source tool, 25

commands
choosing names, 72
choosing names in command suites, 75–76
in command-line invocation, 17–18
testing execution of external, 127–131

completions method, 172

COMPREPLY, 30

config_file method, calling, 97

configuration files
design considerations using, 98
using with command suites, 94–98

configuration, external
about, 89
reading, from files, 90–94

construct %x[], 60

construct library, 191

COPYRIGHT section, meaning of, 51

cri, 189

CSV class, 162

CSV format, organizing output using, 66, 85

CSV-formatted data, reading, 160

Ctrl-C keystroke, stopping apps using, 69

Cucumber, 78–79
installing, 121–123
languages supported by, 119
requirement to do backup, 127
RSpec Book on, 119
running tests, 123–124
tags feature of Cucumber, 130
testing via rake features, 133
understanding, 119–121
use of color in, 154
using Before and After methods with, 126

cut command, in UNIX, 65–66

D

data, encapsulating into classes, 147

database_name, re-creating, 35

default behavior, deciding, 82–86

default values
for app arguments, 79–82
for flags, 41

defaults, reading, from YAML-based configuration file, 92–93

DESCRIPTION section, meaning of, 51

descriptions, adding for command line apps, 36–38

destructive actions, preventing, 82–86

developers, collaborating with other, 109–115

development dependencies, managing, 110–111

distributing apps
with RubyGems, 101–108
using packaging system of operating system, 108–109

dividing code, into multiple files, 141–146

documentation
reusing command-line interface, 50

sorting sections in, 49, 51

writing, 47–50

writing and generating, 112–114

documentation string, 21

documenting
command line arguments, 35–36
command line options, 34–35
command-line interface, 33–38
commands in command suite, 49
options, 49

E

ellipsis, using for multiple arguments, 48

English library
using $CHILD_STATUS with require, 55
using $PROCESS_ID with require, 77

ENV, modifying RUBYLIB inside, 144

env command, 4

ENVIRONMENT section, meaning of, 51

environment variables, 51, 126, 128–129, 181

error, when installing RPM, 109

error messages, using color in, 154

error vs. streams, 59–62

errors, in exit codes, reporting multiple, 57–59

EXAMPLES section, meaning of, 51

executable, 36

execute_command method, 169

exit codes (exit status)
standard, 57
using to report process success or failure, 54–59

exit command, 166

exit_status, reporting multiple errors using, 57–59

expected_filename method, 129

external commands, testing execution of, 127–131

external configuration
about, 89
reading, from files, 90–94

external files, configuring code to find, 142–143

external gem servers, distributing apps through, 105–106

F

factory method, 147
controlling how objects are created using, 148

FakeFS library, 191

File class, basename method, 36

filename method, with ARGF, 80

files, reading external configuration from, 90–94

FILES section, meaning of, 51

flags
applying to to-do list app to set priority, 23
arguments controlling output formatting, 78–79
arguments representing filenames, 77
command line option, 15–16
default value for, 41
default values for, 76–77
documenting arguments to, 49
in main, 183
with optional argument, 21
in OptionParser, 20
with required argument, 21
in thor, 188
unrecognized, 38
-WO flag, 61

formatador library, 190

formatting, output with tables, 159–164

formatting output
based on content, 84–86
to use as input, 63–68

FreeBSD system, 57

G

The Gang of Four, 147

gem command
creating gems with, 104
gemspec relationship to, 102
installing gem locally, 104–105
installing gli app, 26
installing rake, 101
installing ronn app, 43

gem files, packaging code in, 104–105

gem man, as alias for man (footnote), 46

gem man command, 43

gem server, pushing gem to, 105

gem servers
distributing apps through external, 105–106
distributing apps through internal, 106–108

gem terminal-table, 161–162

gem-man page sections, 51

gem-man plug-in
about, 43
installing, 43

gem2rpm, 108

geminabox, setting up and using, 106–108

gems
about, 17
distributing using packaging system of operating system, 108–109
distributing with RubyGems, 101–108

gemsRubyGems, 143

gemspec
adding files from, 142–143
creating, 102–103
using require to import, 103

get_todo_command, 30

getopt option, 18

git control system
command names, 1
functionality of, 16

GitHub, 114–115

GLI
building command suite, 25–31
desc method, 49

help command, 30–31, 39–40
scaffold feature of, 25–30
gli app, installing, 26
global options
applying to to-do list app, 23
in command suites, 17
global variables, *see also* variables
$PROGRAM_NAME, 36
$PROGRAM_NAME, 36
$stdout and $stderr, 64
GNU Project, recommendations for exit codes, 57
Graphical user interfaces (GUIs), vii
grep command, 67

H

help command, 30–31, 34, 39–40
help system, two-level, 38–42
help text, writing, 47–50
highline library, 190
home directory, testing access to home, 125–127
homebrew, OS X package manage, use of color, 155

I

IDEs (integrated development environments), viii
idiomatic UNIX-style interface, creating, 13–23
inabox command, setting up geminabox with, 106–108
input, implementing interactive, 165–173
installing, 197
integrated development environments (IDEs), viii
interactive user interface
libraries for, 190–191
providing, 164–173
internal gem servers, distributing apps through, 106–108
invocation syntax, 48
Is command
about, 166
as alias for "list", 75
expected use case of arguments, 82
output format of, 64

J

Java, command line and growth of, vii–ix
JIRA, 5
working with configuration files, 94–97
JSON browser, implementing, 165–173

K

Katz,Yehuda, 186

L

leading period (.), in filename, 77
lib directory, load path and, 142
LICENSE section, meaning of, 51
Linux distributions, 108
load path
lib directory and, 142
modifying with $LOAD_PATH variable, 144
long-form options
about, 72
naming, 73–75
long-form options, command-line, 14–15
long-form switch, 21
long_desc method, 49

M

main
as alternative to OptionParser, 181–184
using as alternative to command suites, 184–186
main method, 168–169
make_switch method, 20
man (manual) page
alias man to gem man -5 (footnote), 46
including in apps, 42–47
requirement for ".1" in filename, 44
man 3 sysexits, running, 57
managing tasks, 5–10
Markdown plain-text format, 44
methadone, as alternative to OptionParser, 178–181
Mixlib-CLI, 189

Mocha, 135–138
MySQL databases, backing up data app and, 36
mysqldump
about (footnote), 59
handling errors from, 61
output, 63
verifying if exists, 54–55

N

names, choosing option and command, 72–76
namespacing classes, 145
naming commands, in command suites, 17
naming files, by full classname, 145
negatable long-form switch, 21
nroff format, 42

O

one record per line rule, 66
open source app, managing, 114–115
open source applications, gem server for, 105
open source tools
discovering, 191
gem-man plug-in, 43
for parsing command-suite interface, 25
Open3 class
accessing output and error streams, 60–61
in Ruby 1.8 and Ruby 1.9.2, 62
Open4 class, *vs.* Open3 class, 62
operating systems, supported by Aruba, 122
operators
& (ampersand), 58
' (backtick), 60
|=, 58
OptionParser
accept method on, 24
alternatives to using, 176–184
Arrays in, 24, 38
banner, 35, 37
building command-line interface using, 18–23
parameters to on, 21
Regexp support in, 24

response to -h and –help, 34

type conversions in, 24

using square brackets ([]), 48

using with no options, 168

options
    choosing names, 72–75
    command-line, 14–15
    documenting, 49

OPTIONS section, meaning of, 51

optitron, 190

organizing code, within files, 143–146

OS X package manager, homebrew, use of color, 155

output
    adding color using ANSI escape sequences, 155–159
    formatting one record per line, 66–67
    formatting with tables, 159–164
    organizing output using, 66, 85
    using color in reporting status, 154

output vs. error streams, 59–62

P

packaging code, in gem file, 104–105

paint library, 190

parameters, to on, interpretation of, 20–21

parse!, calling, 38

parsers, 189–190

Pivotal Tracker, 5

plumbing commands, 1

porcelain commands, 1

POSIX standard, 69

Pouzin, Louis, 78

principles for common tasks
    making uncommon tasks possible, 74–82
    on not being destructive by default, 82–86
    summary of, 86–87

printing option, 68

process status, using exit codes to determine, 54–59

progress_bar library, 191

projects
    collaborating with developers, 109–111
    providing documentation with, 112–114

puts method, 59
    sending output to STDOUT, 61

R

rails, 17

rainbow library, adding color using, 155–159

rake, 25, 104, 110

rake features, 133

rake test, 137–138

Rakefile, 104, 123, 133

.rc suffix
    configuration structured as YAML using, 92
    using, 78

RDoc, 110, 112–114

read_todo method, 10

reading
    CSV-formatted data, 160
    defaults from YAML-based configuration file, 92–93
    external configuration from files, 90–94

readline , providing user input with, 164–173

readlines method, on STDIN, 81

README file
    documenting environmental variables in, 129
    importance of, 112, 114

Red Hat, yum distribution system in, 108

refactoring, 131

Regexp, support in OptionParser, 24

regexp, 121

reporting status in output, using color in, 154

require
    array of paths in gemspec, 142–143
    putting all files into single file, 145

using $CHILD_STATUS with, 55

using $PROCESS_ID with, 77

using in creating Rakefile, 104

using to import gemspec, 103

rm command, 82–86

ronn app
    about, 43
    creating man page with, 44–47
    format documentation, 44
    installing, 43

RPM package management system, distributing gems using, 108–109

RSpec application, 78

RSpec Book, on Cucumber, 119

RubyGems
    distributing apps with, 101–108
    gem installing in, 143
    gem-man plug-in, 43

RubyGems.org, distributing gems via, 105–106

RUBYLIB, modifying inside ENV, 144

RUBYOPT variable, 61

RUNCOM command, 78

S

scaffold feature of GLI, building skeleton app with, 25–30

sections in documentation, 49, 51

SEE ALSO section, meaning of, 51

shebang, in UNIX systems, 4

shell variable $?, for examining exit codes, 54–55

short-form options
    about, 72
    command-line, 14
    naming, 73–74

short-form switch, 21

SIGABRT signal, 69

SIGHUP signal, 69

SIGINT signal, 69

Signal module, 69

signals, trapping, 69
SIGQUIT signal, 69
skeleton app, building with GLI, 26–30
slop, 190
sort command, in UNIX, 65
[] (square bracket), documenting options using, 48
square brackets ([ ]), using to document argument to flag, 49
standard error stream
    about, 59
    accessing, 60–61
standard input stream, 79
standard output stream, 59
status, using color in output reporting, 154
STDERR constant
    sending output to streams, 61–62
    vs.$stderr, 64
STDIN
    readlines method on, 81
    standard input and, 80
STDOUT constant
    calling tty?, 85
    sending output to streams, 61–62
    vs.$stdout, 64
strategy pattern, organizing multiple ways of doing something, 149–151
stubbing, 135–136
switches
    applying to to-do list app to set priority, 23
    command line option, 15–16
    in main, 183
    in OptionParser, 20
    in thor, 188
    unrecognized, 38
SYNOPSIS section, meaning of, 51
sysexits, 57
system, modifying, 82

T

tab completion, in to-do list app, 30–31
tables, formatting output with tables, 159–164
task management, 5–10

term-ansicolor library, 155, 191
terminal-table, 161–162
Test Driven Development (Beck), 139
Test-Driven Development (TDD), 139
testing
    access to home directory, 125–127
    complex behavior, 125–127
    execution of external commands, 127–131
    installing Cucumber and Aruba, 121–123
    libraries, 191
    running Cucumber tests, 123–124
    running unit tests, 131–139
    understanding Cucumber and Aruba, 119–121
    understanding acceptance tests, 118–119
    using acceptance tests, 118–131
thor
    open source tool, 25
    using as alternative to command suites, 186–189
to-do list app
    using main as alternative to command suites, 184–186
    using thor as alternative to command suites, 187–189
todo list app
    acceptance testing using Cucumber and Aruba, 119–121
    adding attributes to classes, 147
    adding code to find external files, 142–143
    adding help system, 39
    building command-suite interface, 23–31
    creating, 6–11
    creating a gemspec to use with, 102–103
    designing output to use as input, 65–68
    extracting units from existing code, 131–133

formatting output as tables, 160–164
maintaining code, 146
modifying RUBYLIB inside ENV, 144
naming commands, 75–76
running Cucumber tests, 123–124
setting up Rakefile, 133–134
testing access to home directory, 125–127
using color in, 155–159
using configuration files with, 94–98
using factory method to control creation of objects, 148
using require to put files into single file, 145
using standard input stream as default, 81–82
using strategy pattern, 149–151
writing unit tests, 135–139
TODO_FILE constant, 10
trap method, 69
trapping signals from other apps, 68–69
trollop, as alternative to OptionParser, 176–178
trouble-ticket system, 5
tty?, calling, 85
two-level help system, 38–42
type conversions, in OptionParser, 24

U

unit tests, 131–139
UNIX
    about RUNCOM command, 78
    awk command in, 66–67
    bash, vii, 30
    creating idiomatic-style interface, 13–23
    cut command in, 65–66
    format of directory, 63–64
    man (manual page) in apps, 42
    POSIX standard in, 69
    rm command, 82–86
    section 1 of man (manual) system, 44

sort command in, 65
TTY in, 85
user interface, 164
using .rc suffix, 78
"The UNIX Way", 64
user input, providing with
readline, 164–173
user interfaces, libraries for
user interfaces, 190–191
users, generating configuration file for, 93–94
using configuration files with,
94–98

V

variables, 64
$?, for examining exit
codes, 54–55
$CHILD_STATUS, using
with require, 55
$LOAD_PATH, 103, 133,
144

$PROCESS_ID, using
with require, 77
$PROGRAM_NAME, us-
ing in banner, 36
$stderr*vs.* STDERR con-
stant, 64
$stdout*vs.* STDOUT con-
stant, 64
VERSION constant, 103
version control, 111
version of apps, changing,
103

W

Wanstrath, Chris, 43
warn method, disabling messages sent with, 61
Windows
POSIX standard in, 69
using Aruba on, 122
write_todo method, 10

writing
documentation, 112–114
help text and documenta-
tion, 47–50
unit tests, 135–139

X

XML *vs.* YAML, 91

Y

YAML
generating configuration
user file, 93–94
storing Ruby objects us-
ing, 95–97
using as configuration file
format, 90–92
vs. XML, 91
yum distribution system, using with RPM, 108

Learn a New Language This Year

Want to be a better programmer? Each new programming language you learn teaches you something new about computing. Come see what you're missing.

You should learn a programming language every year, as recommended by *The Pragmatic Programmer*. But if one per year is good, how about *Seven Languages in Seven Weeks*? In this book you'll get a hands-on tour of Clojure, Haskell, Io, Prolog, Scala, Erlang, and Ruby. Whether or not your favorite language is on that list, you'll broaden your perspective of programming by examining these languages side-by-side. You'll learn something new from each, and best of all, you'll learn how to learn a language quickly.

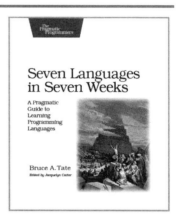

Bruce A. Tate
(328 pages) ISBN: 9781934356593. $34.95
http://pragprog.com/titles/btlang

Bill Karwin has helped thousands of people write better SQL and build stronger relational databases. Now he's sharing his collection of antipatterns—the most common errors he's identified out of those thousands of requests for help.

Most developers aren't SQL experts, and most of the SQL that gets used is inefficient, hard to maintain, and sometimes just plain wrong. This book shows you all the common mistakes, and then leads you through the best fixes. What's more, it shows you what's *behind* these fixes, so you'll learn a lot about relational databases along the way.

Bill Karwin
(352 pages) ISBN: 9781934356555. $34.95
http://pragprog.com/titles/bksqla

Testing is only the beginning

Start with Test Driven Development, Domain Driven Design, and Acceptance Test Driven Planning in Ruby. Then add Shoulda, Cucumber, Factory Girl, and Rcov for the ultimate in Ruby and Rails development.

Behaviour-Driven Development (BDD) gives you the best of Test Driven Development, Domain Driven Design, and Acceptance Test Driven Planning techniques, so you can create better software with self-documenting, executable tests that bring users and developers together with a common language.

Get the most out of BDD in Ruby with *The RSpec Book*, written by the lead developer of RSpec, David Chelimsky.

David Chelimsky, Dave Astels, Zach Dennis, Aslak Hellesøy, Bryan Helmkamp, Dan North
(448 pages) ISBN: 9781934356371. $38.95
http://pragprog.com/titles/achbd

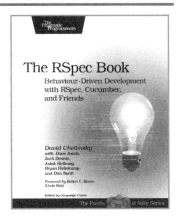

Rails Test Prescriptions is a comprehensive guide to testing Rails applications, covering Test-Driven Development from both a theoretical perspective (why to test) and from a practical perspective (how to test effectively). It covers the core Rails testing tools and procedures for Rails 2 and Rails 3, and introduces popular add-ons, including RSpec, Shoulda, Cucumber, Factory Girl, and Rcov.

Noel Rappin
(368 pages) ISBN: 9781934356647. $34.95
http://pragprog.com/titles/nrtest

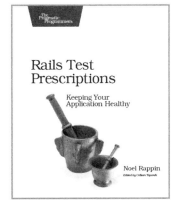

Go Beyond with Rails and NoSQL

There's so much new to learn with Rails 3 and the latest crop of NoSQL databases. These titles will get you up to speed on the latest.

Thousands of developers have used the first edition of *Rails Recipes* to solve the hard problems. Now, five years later, it's time for the Rails 3.1 edition of this trusted collection of solutions, completely revised by Rails master Chad Fowler.

Chad Fowler
(350 pages) ISBN: 9781934356777. $35
http://pragprog.com/titles/rr2

Data is getting bigger and more complex by the day, and so are your choices in handling it. From traditional RDBMS to newer NoSQL approaches, *Seven Databases in Seven Weeks* takes you on a tour of some of the hottest open source databases today. In the tradition of Bruce A. Tate's *Seven Languages in Seven Weeks*, this book goes beyond a basic tutorial to explore the essential concepts at the core of each technology.

Eric Redmond and Jim Wilson
(330 pages) ISBN: 9781934356920. $35
http://pragprog.com/titles/rwdata

What you Need to Know

Each new version of the Web brings its own gold rush. Here are your tools.

HTML5 and CSS3 are the future of web development, but you don't have to wait to start using them. Even though the specification is still in development, many modern browsers and mobile devices already support HTML5 and CSS3. This book gets you up to speed on the new HTML5 elements and CSS3 features you can use right now, and backwards compatible solutions ensure that you don't leave users of older browsers behind.

Brian P. Hogan
(280 pages) ISBN: 9781934356685. $33
http://pragprog.com/titles/bhh5

Modern web development takes more than just HTML and CSS with a little JavaScript mixed in. Clients want more responsive sites with faster interfaces that work on multiple devices, and you need the latest tools and techniques to make that happen. This book gives you more than 40 concise, tried-and-true solutions to today's web development problems, and introduces new workflows that will expand your skillset.

Brian P. Hogan, Chris Warren, Mike Weber, Chris Johnson, Aaron Godin
(344 pages) ISBN: 9781934356838. $35
http://pragprog.com/titles/wbdev

Welcome to the Better Web

You need a better JavaScript and more expressive CSS and HTML today. Start here.

CoffeeScript is JavaScript done right. It provides all of JavaScript's functionality wrapped in a cleaner, more succinct syntax. In the first book on this exciting new language, CoffeeScript guru Trevor Burnham shows you how to hold onto all the power and flexibility of JavaScript while writing clearer, cleaner, and safer code.

Trevor Burnham
(160 pages) ISBN: 9781934356784. $29
http://pragprog.com/titles/tbcoffee

CSS is fundamental to the web, but it's a basic language and lacks many features. Sass is just like CSS, but with a whole lot of extra power so you can get more done, more quickly. Build better web pages today with *Pragmatic Guide to Sass*. These concise, easy-to-digest tips and techniques are the shortcuts experienced CSS developers need to start developing in Sass today.

Hampton Catlin and Michael Lintorn Catlin
(128 pages) ISBN: 9781934356845. $25
http://pragprog.com/titles/pg_sass

Advanced Ruby and Rails

What used to be the realm of experts is fast becoming the stuff of day-to-day development. Jump to the head of the class in Ruby and Rails.

Rails 3 is a huge step forward. You can now easily extend the framework, change its behavior, and replace whole components to bend it to your will, all without messy hacks. This pioneering book is the first resource that deep dives into the new Rails 3 APIs and shows you how to use them to write better web applications and make your day-to-day work with Rails more productive.

José Valim
(184 pages) ISBN: 9781934356739. $33
http://pragprog.com/titles/jvrails

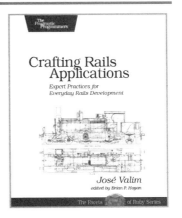

As a Ruby programmer, you already know how much fun it is. Now see how to unleash its power, digging under the surface and exploring the language's most advanced features: a collection of techniques and tricks known as *metaprogramming*. Once the domain of expert Rubyists, metaprogramming is now accessible to programmers of all levels—from beginner to expert. *Metaprogramming Ruby* explains metaprogramming concepts in a down-to-earth style and arms you with a practical toolbox that will help you write great Ruby code.

Paolo Perrotta
(296 pages) ISBN: 9781934356470. $32.95
http://pragprog.com/titles/ppmetr

The Pragmatic Bookshelf

The Pragmatic Bookshelf features books written by developers for developers. The titles continue the well-known Pragmatic Programmer style and continue to garner awards and rave reviews. As development gets more and more difficult, the Pragmatic Programmers will be there with more titles and products to help you stay on top of your game.

Visit Us Online

This Book's Home Page
http://pragprog.com/titles/dccar
Source code from this book, errata, and other resources. Come give us feedback, too!

Register for Updates
http://pragprog.com/updates
Be notified when updates and new books become available.

Join the Community
http://pragprog.com/community
Read our weblogs, join our online discussions, participate in our mailing list, interact with our wiki, and benefit from the experience of other Pragmatic Programmers.

New and Noteworthy
http://pragprog.com/news
Check out the latest pragmatic developments, new titles and other offerings.

Save on the eBook

Save on the eBook versions of this title. Owning the paper version of this book entitles you to purchase the electronic versions at a terrific discount.

PDFs are great for carrying around on your laptop—they are hyperlinked, have color, and are fully searchable. Most titles are also available for the iPhone and iPod touch, Amazon Kindle, and other popular e-book readers.

Buy now at *http://pragprog.com/coupon*

Contact Us

Online Orders:	*http://pragprog.com/catalog*
Customer Service:	*support@pragprog.com*
International Rights:	*translations@pragprog.com*
Academic Use:	*academic@pragprog.com*
Write for Us:	*http://pragprog.com/write-for-us*
Or Call:	+1 800-699-7764